STEAM and RAIL in INDONESIA

Jack Rozendaal

A Locomotives International Publication

Above: Making its way down the main street in Madiun on 5th August 1983 is B5012, a wood-fired 2-4-0 built by Sharp Stewart nearly a century earlier in 1884. Photo: Keith R. Chester.

Front Cover: 'Siantar' class 2-8-4T locomotive no. 48 of the Deli Railway Company seen at Tebing Tinggi on 31st May 1978. By this date the Deli Railway had been absorbed into the PJKA, Indonesian State Railways. Photo: Uwe Bergmann.

Rear Cover: Sudhono Sugar Mill no. 6, a 600 mm gauge Engerth 0-6+4 built by Arn. Jung (3625/1925). Photo: Ray Gardiner.

Title Page: Early postcards from Soerabaja of a sugar plantation and mill, thought to be Krobis Baru Rejoagung, showing an Orenstein & Koppel 0-4-4-0T Mallet, one of several supplied c. 1909-10. Views courtesy of Chistopher Walker.

ISBN 1-900340-11-9
First Edition. Published by Paul Catchpole Ltd., The Old School House, Arrow, Alcester, Warwickshire, B49 5PJ, England
e-mail: locomotives.international@talk21.com   Internet home page: http://www.stargate-uk.co.uk/locomotives-international

Edited and typeset by Paul Catchpole, printed and bound by Spectrum Digital Imaging, Walsall, England.
British Library Cataloguing in Publication Data. A catalogue record for this book is available from the British Library.

Steam and Rail in Indonesia
Jack Rozendaal

Contents

Additional Credits:
A number of eminent people have contributed illustrations to this publication and their names are given in the photo captions. Particular thanks are due to Jim Grant, not only for providing a colour section illustrating the preserved locomotives at Ambarawa, but also for the introductory overview of Indonesian railway history.

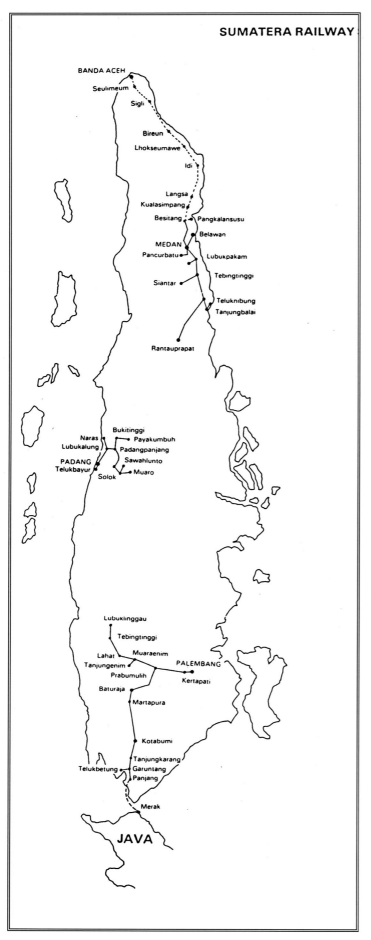

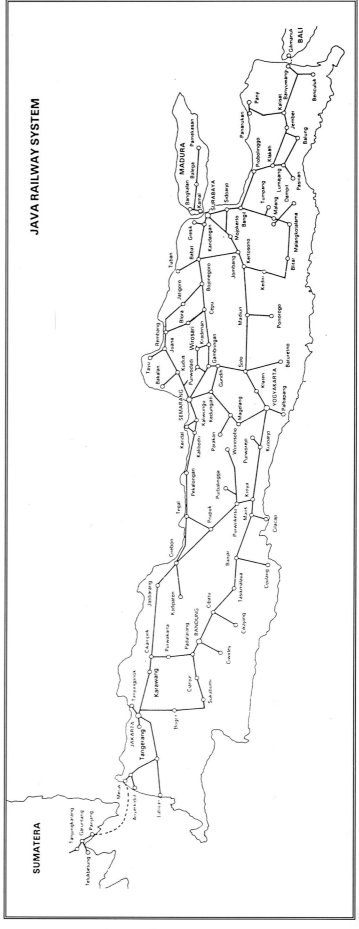

Railways in Indonesia

Indonesia's first railway line was laid in 1864 between Semerang and Tanggung, a distance of 15 miles (24km) of 4'8½" standard gauge track, opened on 10th August 1867. By 1872 it had been extended to Surakarta and Yogyakarta, however, the standard gauge was not generally adopted and when additional track was being laid in the 1870s, 3'6" (1.067m), and some 1'11½" (600 mm), became the dominant format. In the mid 1890s track was laid which linked Jakarta with Surabaya and a third rail was laid on the standard gauge Semerang-Yogyakarta track in 1899 to allow through running.

At its peak there were 3,500 miles (5,640 km) of track, much of which was laid by private companies, however, by the late 1930s more than half of the system was under the control of the Netherlands Indies Railways. As a result of the multiplicity of owners there was an equal variety of locomotive types. By 1930 the main line system was modern and well organised, with powerful, advanced locomotives operated by Nederlands Indische Spoorweg Maatshappij (N.I.S.), and the state railway company Staats Spoorwegen (S.S.).

When the Japanese arrived they stripped Java of its standard gauge locomotives and rolling stock and transferred these to the Manchurian railway system. With the effects of the Japanese occupation between 1942 and 1945, the War of Independence that followed, and the shortage of capital following independence, the railway system had to rely on vintage steam locomotives and ageing rolling stock long after normal expectancy. It says much for the state of the country's pre-war equipment that it was still operating with a degree of efficiency 40 years later. The original private enterprise companies required small and light locomotives and a large variety of these were imported. The main lines were served by compound Pacifics, with 4-6-4s and 2-12-2Ts for heavy freight runs. Post war, 1950/51, when the Indonesian Government took over the system, one hundred D52 Class 2-8-2s were purchased from Krupp and these remained in service until the 1970s.

Sumatra had its own variety of locomotives which differed from anything on Java, grouped mainly on the south end of the island and at Medan and Aceh in the north. Madura also had a short network until recently. The oldest line was the Atjeh Tramway built to 750 mm gauge in north east Sumatra, the first section of which opened in 1876. The NV Deli Spoorveg Maatschappij (D.S.M.), which connected with the Atjeh Tramway, started running in 1886 and operated 59 steam locomotives and one petrol powered model on track of 3'6" gauge (1.067m) over 338 miles (544km). On the west side of Sumatra a network of S.S. lines was built up to serve a coal mining area, the first section having opened in 1891. The S.S. lines in the south of Sumatra opened as late as 1914 but are now more significant as the coal mining has declined.

The lines in Java were nationalised in 1942 during the occupation becoming the Djawatan Kerata Api and locomotives were renumbered according to the Japanese system - a letter for the number of coupled axles followed by two numbers for the class and then the running number. In 1954 D.K.A. operated over 2,876 miles (4,629 km) of 3'6" gauge track and 60 miles (96 km) of 60m on Java. On Sumatra the mileages were 348 miles (560 km) of 3'6" gauge, 330 miles (536 km) of 2'5½" gauge (750 mm) and 196 miles (317 km) of 600 mm gauge. By 1958 the D.K.A. were operating 917 steam, 13 electric and 27 diesel locomotives on the 3'6" gauge in Java. In Sumatra there were 34 steam locomotives on the 750 mm gauge, and 17 on 600 mm. When the Sumatran systems were incorporated into the nationalised railways in 1963 the initials changed to P.N.K.A. (Perusahaan Negara Kerata Api - State Enterprise Railway).

By the mid 1960s the railways were in a poor financial position but since then the Indonesian Government has implemented plans to restore the P.N.K.A. to its position as the major land transportation company on Java. In 1969 a five year plan allowed for the disposal of 200 steam locomotives more than 60 years old and their replacement over the period. Track and bridges were also to be refurbished or replaced. Ten years later 392 steam locomotives were still on the books but only 173 were still in service. This represented a figure of 44% available for use as compared to 70% of available diesels on the books. In 1973 the P.N.K.A. was renamed the P.J.K.A. - Perusahaan Jawatan Kereta Api.

Today there are 4,967 kilometres of track on Java and 1,491 on Sumatra. Now titled 'PERMUKA' Perusahaan Umun Kerata Api, the railway company has pulled itself up out of the doldrums of the early 1980s and the system has been revitalised by the general economic upswing on Java. Figures for 1992 showed that 66 million journeys were made.

Although steam has now gone, travelling by train in Indonesia is still an experience particularly by 'Bisnis', middle of the range comfort, or 'Ekonimi' third class. The former uses newer carriages, provides a meal service and, on longer journeys, an additional cushion which you can either sit on or lean against according to your desire. 'Ekonomi' is older carriages and harder seats but still with lots of leg room as opposed to the sardine cans which pass for buses. Surprisingly despite their leisurely rate of travel and frequent stops they match and occasionally surpass the rate of progress of the competing buses which threaten to destroy the local services.

Place Names

Over time the spelling of place names has changed. For the most part the author has used the versions familiar to him when he lived there, which are not necessarily the current versions. The Dutch colonial 'oe' has changed to 'u', and 'tj' has changed to 'c', so Cepu might formerly have been seen written as Tjepoe. The 'dj' changed to 'j' and then the 'j' or 'i' became a 'y', for instance as in Djocdjakarta, Jogjakarta, Yogyakarta.

Some place names have changed completely. Three that feature prominently in this book are the capitol Batavia, which became Jakarta, Willem I, now Ambarawa, and Jack Rozendaal's home town of Solo, today known as Surakarta (Soerakarta).

Introduction

Batavia, Trams, and Steam Locomotives

The writer started observing steam trains from a very early age. It was so, that the parents proceeded to the then Dutch East Indies in 1921, where the head of the family took up a post in the teaching profession and settled in the then capital of the East Indies, Batavia (now Jakarta), the so called the 'Queen of the East'.

Batavia by 1881 boasted a tramway, at first horse-drawn and later converted into a steam tram using fireless locomotives of the 0-4-0 wheel arrangement. These fireless locomotives drew their steam from a centrally situated boiler house. It was there that this toddler caught his first glimpse of a steam engine, albeit a tram locomotive, as the tramway ran along the front of the house. These tram engines could travel distances lasting about one hour, but what happened when an engine ran out of steam and hot water the writer cannot tell. The system was abandoned in 1930 when the tramway was electrified. It is on record that one of the engines suffered a boiler explosion whilst being charged.

Batavia's Tramway Chronology

Pre 1881   Horse drawn trams
1881   Formation of the Nederlandisch-Indische Tramweg
            Maatschappij (N.I.T.M.)
            (Netherland-Indies Tramway Company)

1882-1909 Introduction of fireless 0-4-0 locomotives nos. 1 to 21
1921   Introduction of coal fired 0-4-0 locomotives numbers 51 to 67
1930   Amalgamation of the N.I.T.M. and B.E.T. (Batavia Electric Tramway).
            Electrification of N.I.T.M. lines.
1933   Cessation of fireless steam locomotive services
1934   Cessation of coal fired steam locomotive services
1964   Cessation of electric tram services in Jakarta

Shortly after arrival my parents moved to Sukabumi, a pleasant little town in the cool Preanger Highlands. There are vivid recollections of the Batavia - Sukabumi - Bandung Express thundering over high viaducts spanning deep ravines. In those early days (1926), one travelled by train.

In Sukabumi, Dad once took me to the station where a glimpse was caught of a 2-6-6-0 Mallet tank locomotive which had just arrived with its train. Now the youngster was hooked on steam for ever! The then State Railways (Staats Spoorwegen, abbreviated S.S.) used mainly Mallet compounds on the steeply graded Preanger Mountain lines of West Java. Western Java's Preanger Mountains of volcanic origin caused the early railway builders many headaches. Earthquakes, landslides and flash floods were common occurrences. The lines abounded with many viaducts, sharp curves and heavy gradients and it is no wonder that the heaviest locomotives on the system could be found here.

A two-cylinder coal fired 0-4-0 tram locomotive of the Netherlands-Indies Tramway Company built to 1,188mm gauge by Hohenzollern.
Photo: author's collection.

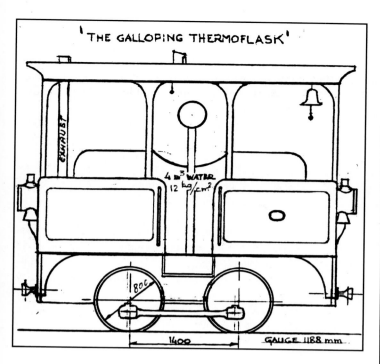

'THE GALLOPING THERMOFLASK'

Above: 'The Galloping Thermoflask' was a two-cylinder fireless tram locomotive built by Hohenzollern. The pressure vessel held 4 cubic metres of water and worked at a maximum pressure of 12 atmospheres. The cylinder diameter x stroke was 380 x 400 mm. Drg: J.R.

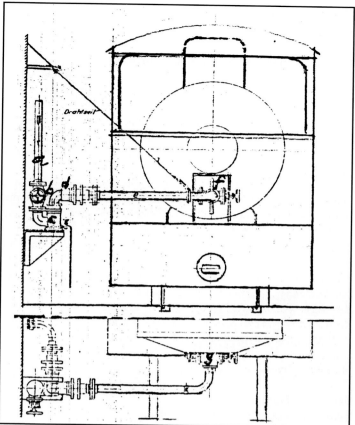

Above: Diagram of a boiler filling station showing boiler charging from in front and above.
a=steam supply,
b=stop valve,
c=swivel joint,
d=ball joint,
f=screw connector,
g=loco stop valve.
Drg: J.R.

Left: A Batavia City electric tram with two trailers, the nearest one open but with a corrugated iron roof.
Photo: author's collection.

These mountain lines were initially worked by 2-6-0 two-cylinder compound tank locomotives which could not cope for long with the steadily increasing train loads of the time. Shortly after the turn of the century the 0-4-4-2 Mallet compound tank loco was introduced, followed by the 2-6-6-0 Mallet compound tank a couple of years later, and culminating in the 2-8-8-0 Mallet compound tender locomotive of 1916, the largest locomotives ever on the Javan State Railways. However, after initially experiencing problems with the steam tightness of flexible joints on the preceding Mallet classes, the administration opted for the less complex rigid framed and two-cylindered simple expansion locomotive again and the 12-coupled 'Javanic' type came into being. Although successful, the severity of the Preanger curves caused heavy flange wear on the leading coupled wheels and the Mallet system was re-adopted for heavy mountain service, thus finally the big 2-8-8-0 and a more modern 2-6-6-0 evolved. The

Right: One of the 2-6-0 tank engines crossing a steel viaduct in the Preanger Mountains with a goods train.
Photo: author's collection.

Below: A Mallet compound 2-6-6-0T negotiates a section of newly laid track following a landslip in the Preanger Mountains.
Photo: author's collection.

Below: Electric State Railways 2-4-4-2 1,500 Volts DC electric locomotive no. 9002.
Photo: van Felde, author's collection.

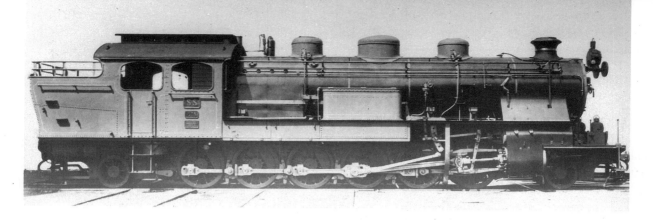

S.S. 'Javanic' 2-12-2T no. 818, later PJKA F1018, built by Werkspoor (373/1915). Works photo courtesy of Ian G.T. Duncan.

'Javanics' then saw further service in other mountainous regions with less severe curvature.

Electrification

In 1925 the electrification of the lines in and around Batavia on the 1,500 Volts dc system was completed and later extended to Buitenzorg, now renamed Bogor, the erstwhile seat of the Viceroy of the East Indies. Plans were afoot to extend the electrification to Sukabumi but these never materialised. My parents became acquainted with the Resident Engineer on the electrification project and the author met this eminent Electrical Engineer again after fifteen years when enrolling in a Technical College, due to him being the Principal of the College.

For express trains the type 1B+B1 and 1A-AA-A1 of 1,570 and 1,500 horse power were introduced with maximum speeds of 90 kph. The all adhesion bogie electric locomotive was still to come. For mixed trains 1,200 hp and 900 hp locomotives of different wheel notations were introduced. For suburban services the E.M.U. was introduced and for shunting purposes battery-electric locomotives were used.

The electrified railways were called 'Electrische Staats Spoorwegen', abbreviated to ESS (Electric State Railways), but steam still frequented the capital of Batavia, the youthful writer de-training a few times from the Surabaya - Batavia 'Day Express' at Weltvreden Station when the family was on its way on furlough to the Mother Country (Holland). A Swiss designed 'Pacific', one of the author's pet engines, mostly did the honours on the last stretch of the day long journey from central Java in those far off days. The then 900 km journey from Surabaya to Batavia and vice verse in the 1930s was entirely steam hauled. After uncoupling, the engine always drove past the arrival plat-form, proceeding to the loco shed. The last picture in this section depicts the above mentioned express of pre-1930 days hauled by one of the celebrated Werkspoor of Amsterdam four-cylinder compound 'Pacific' type locomotives entering Mr. Cornelis (renamed Djatinegara), a pleasant suburb of the otherwise stifling hot Batavia. This picture has some sentimental value, Mr. Cornelis being the birthplace of the author.

A Surabaya - Batavia express entering Meester Cornelis station situated on the outskirts of Batavia. Photo: author's collection.

The 1930s in Solo

The mid and late 1930s were of great interest notwithstanding the Great Depression. It so happened that the family returned to the East Indies in 1928 and settled in Surakarta or Solo, which was a Sultanate. This large town in central Java, lying in a rather hot plain between surrounding extinct volcanoes was at the time a large Railway junction and a veritable steam paradise, with both "Breedspoor" (broad gauge), actually the standard 4'8½" gauge and "Normaal Spoor", or standard gauge, which was in fact the 3'6" Cape Gauge.

The 4'8½" gauge was run by a private railway company called the Nederlandsh Indische Spoorweg Maatschappij (the Netherlands Indies Railway Company, abbreviated N.I.S.), and ran from the Port of Samarang on Java's north coast on the Java Sea via Solo to Jogjakarta, which town was another Sultanate. The N.I.S. railway was the Netherland Indies oldest railway, the first tracks being laid in 1864 from Samarang into the interior. This company before World War 2 also ran an extensive 3'6" network in the form of a tramway from the town of Bojolali through the City of Solo to Baturetno, which was the end of the line, as well as out of Jogjakarta to other towns in central Java. The 3'6" main railway was of course run by the state as their Staats Spoorwegen (S.S.). All the railways on the island of Java were fully developed by the 1930s.

Solo was situated in a sugar cane growing area and the numerous steam worked sugar plantation railways added greatly to the grand steam scene. The place could be stifling hot in the wet Monsoon but the invitingly cool hill stations on the slopes of the surrounding volcanoes were only a few hours drive away by car. One of the twin volcanoes west of the town called the Merapi and Merbabu was active. The volcano Merapi, or "Fire Mountain", was notorious for its sudden eruptions, sending clouds of incandescent matter down its populated slopes and ravines killing all living things in its path. The author can recollect the eruption of 1930 which killed over 2,000 people, the ash rain shrouding the town in a two day long twilight and blanketing it with a thick layer of volcanic ash.

Solo boasted four railway stations, a Central Station called Balapan served by the N.I.S. 4'8½" and 3'6" gauges and the S.S. 3'6" gauge, a city tram station called Solo-Kotta (Solo-City) served by the 3'6" tramline, and two outlying stations. The one named Purwosari was served by the N.I.S. 3'6" gauge tram line and the 4'8½" gauge, (the 3'6" gauge line circumventing this station), and the Djèbrès station serving the 3'6" gauge main line. Once upon a time this last station was also served by a 3'6" gauge tram line originating from near Solo-Kotta station, giving access from the Sultan's Palace (Kraton) in the centre of the city to Djèbrès station, as this latter station was laid out on ground kindly ceded to the S.S. by His Highness. However, this connection was taken up before the writer's time as now the Sultan would move around by automobile. Besides being a Sultanate and a large railway junction Solo was also a garrison town with a gem of a 17th Century European military style fortification, Fort Vredenburgh,

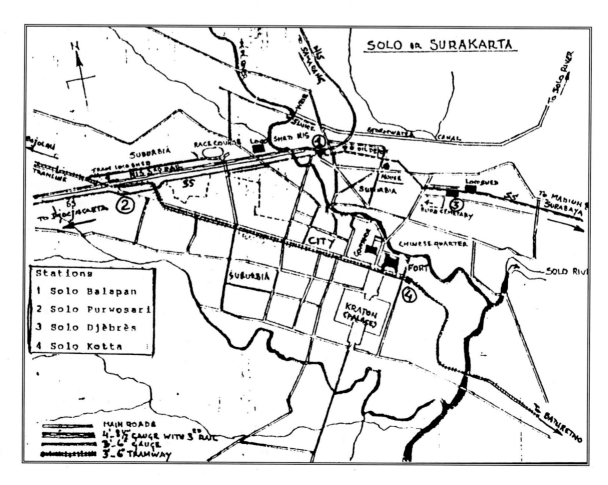

A works photograph of Staats Spoorwegen no. 380, a two cylinder Pacific built by SLM. Photo courtesy of C.J. Walker.

S.S. four cylinder compound Pacific no. 1003, a Werkspoor product. Photo courtesy of C.J. Walker.

as well as being the administrative capital of Central Java.

The State Railways 3'6" gauge main line connecting the administrative capital of Batavia with the commercial capital of Surabaya, which was also a port, ran through Solo. This railway was of class 1 standard. There was a second through connection along Java's north coast but this was of class 2 standard and required passengers to change trains. Once a day an express train ran vice verse between the two cities during daylight hours. This was the "Één Daagse" (Daylight Express), calling at Solo at 10 a.m. Batavia bound and at 3 p.m. Surabaya bound. The journey of 900 km took the entire day and the maximum speed was 100 km/hour on the plains and 65 km/hour on the hilly sections, this pre-war express being reputedly the fastest in South-East Asia. In the late thirties a night express was laid on between the two cities to cater for businessmen as air services were in their infancy. The average speed of this night express was somewhat slower than the day express in order not to arrive too early at the destination. The honours were mainly done by the celebrated Werkspoor four-cylinder compound 4-6-2 Pacific on the level stretch in West Java and by a (rebuilt) Swiss built two-cylinder Pacific with a "Javanic" 2-12-2T two-cylinder tank locomotive on the hill section.

Needless to say that on many occasions the author hung around the main station in the blazing tropical heat of the day to witness the arrival and departure of these expresses and sometimes the comings and goings of the 11 pm night express Batavia bound. The clerestory roofed coaching stock on these expresses at the time were of composite build with wood on a steel skeleton and were 18 metres long with vestibules on each end, a central isle, and bellow connections between the coaches. They were vacuum braked and electrically lit, with electric fans to keep the passengers cool in the tropical heat. Air conditioning was only to come in the late thirties. The coaches of the newly laid on night express were of all steel construction and were air conditioned from the outset. These coaches rode on S.S. designed two-axle bogies. Dining cars were provided on these expresses, with snow white linen, flowers and monogrammed crockery and cutlery. The kitchen served à la carte meals, a far cry from today's tasteless, pre-cooked and deep frozen pedestrian fare.

Coaching stock was all built by the S.S. in their Mangarai Workshops at Meester Cornelis, a suburb of Batavia. Mangarai was a former steam workshop but steam repairs were now concentrated in Madiun. Coach interiors made at Mangarai were teak panelled, the coach windows being provided with three sliding panels, one of glass, one of wire mesh to keep the grit out, and one being louvered to keep the monsoon rain out. Seats were leather upholstered for coolness.

As regards the express locomotives briefly mentioned before, the Swiss-designed class 700 Pacific introduced in 1911 was really the first large express passenger locomotive on the system. These locos were the writer's favourite engines at the time and in his opinion the best looking ones on the system, but as the saying goes, beauty is in the eye of the beholder. When the author knew them in the mid and late thirties they were ageing dowagers and were nominated to be replaced, but with the Great Depression showing signs of abating the Javan state railways, like every-where else, got caught up in the great rail speed-up of that period. The engines could not therefore be missed and went through a rejuvenating spell when the front end and inner firebox were improved. They were given enlarged stove pipe chimneys and smoke deflectors, which in the writer's opinion improved their looks. On test runs they easily reached 120 km per hour and hauled the Day and Night Expresses on the more level stretch between the capital, Batavia, and Tji-Kampek. One of the photographs depicts engine no. 711 giving cause for a celebration, the locomotive having reeled off more than 100,000 km with the same set of improved big end bearings.

With express trains getting heavier all the time there was a need for a still larger and more powerful engine and the celebrated Werkspoor built four-cylinder compound Pacific appeared on the scene. They were wholly Dutch designed and built and were for years the showpiece of the Javan State Railways and were regarded as one of the fastest 3'6" gauge steam locomotives ever built, being capable of speeds in excess of 120 km per hour. However, they had their shortcomings such as a lack of adjustable axlebox wedges (an omission) and were initially somewhat sensi-tive to track elevation deficiencies. Also the lack of side control springs on the rear running axle made running at speed somehow 'lively', as born out by an acquaintance of the time who once had a cab ride on one of these locomotives. An unexpected lurch of the engine at speed threw him right across the cab. For a long time a debate raged amongst the railway fraternity questioning the wisdom of having a locomotive designed from scratch when proven designs could be had 'off the shelf' from the established locomotive manufacturers. Nevertheless they gave yeoman service and also underwent a rejuvenating spell. When the front end was improved and smoke deflectors fitted they were made suitable for running at sustained speeds of 100 km per hour.

For years the author observed these latter Pacifics heading the Expresses, and getting away with a heavy express was always a sight to behold. Invariably the engine, with open cylinder cocks, had to 'set back' once or twice when the receiver relief valve suddenly opened up in forward, followed by a thunderous slip shooting a billowing cloud of smoke high up in the air, but once up to speed they went like the wind. Having no exterior by-pass valves on the outside low pressure cylinders but having snifter valves on the cylinder covers, these locomotives had that charac-teristic sound of cylinders exhaling when coasting.

What Could Have Been

As the years progressed, compounding on the Javan S.S. system became out of vogue and simpling of these Pacific loco-motives was being considered. In 1930 Werkspoor of Amsterdam,

No. 711, an SLM Pacific garlanded with flowers and attended by men in white suits for a special occassion.
Photo: author's collection.

as well as the locomotive manufacturing firm of Borsig in Germany, prepared the plans for these latter Pacifics to be altered into simple expansion locomotives, however, the onset of the Great Depression at the end of the twenties put paid to these plans and the project was shelved. Shortly after the War the writer was employed by Werkspoor in Amsterdam in their ship propulsion design department but never managed to find out how these loco-motives would look like after the reconstruction and what it would of entailed. This was probably due to the post-war State Department of Overseas Possessions still being "de facto" in power during the clamour for independence, and customers' plans could therefore not be revealed. Knowing the thrifty Dutch, however, much of the locomotive would have been re-used in the reconstruction.

As these locomotives had composite framing, which in the compound version never gave any trouble, this foundation would have been retained unaltered. The crank axle as such never gave any trouble in the compound version and would also have been retained, as would the four connecting rods and the remainder of the motion, unaltered. Most likely the inside cylinders would have been either rebored or re-sleeved, and there would then remain the fitting of new outside cylinder castings of reduced bore. The loco-motive would then be a four-cylinder simple expansion engine, in looks hardly distinguishable from the compound version. Probably a Kylchap duplex exhaust would be fitted to soften the exhaust blast as the Javan steam locomotive could be a notorious grit thrower on account of the type of "soft" coal used. This device was very much in vogue in the late twenties and early thir-ties after its introduction by André Chapelon, however, the above is conjecture. These Pacifics were constructed as compounds and finally dismantled as compounds, and would have been the final express locomotives on the Javan system had not the ensuing Pacific War intervened, as early dieselisation was on the cards and also taking into account that the supply of good locomotive fuel on the system had always been problematic.

Keith Chester visited Solo Balapan shed in later years. 0-4-0 B5212 (Hartmann 3562/1912), observed on 9th August 1983, was retained for railfan tours, but also still saw use for local trip and shunting work. Photo: Keith R. Chester.

Four cylinder compound Pacific C5313 built by Werkspoor in 1921 with inside high pressure and outside low pressure cylinders, all driving on the leading coupled axle. The picture was taken in 1971 and shows another four cylinder compound behind, a class CC50 2-6-6-0 Mallet. Photo: A.E. Durrant.

The 3'6" (1067 mm) Gauge State Railways System

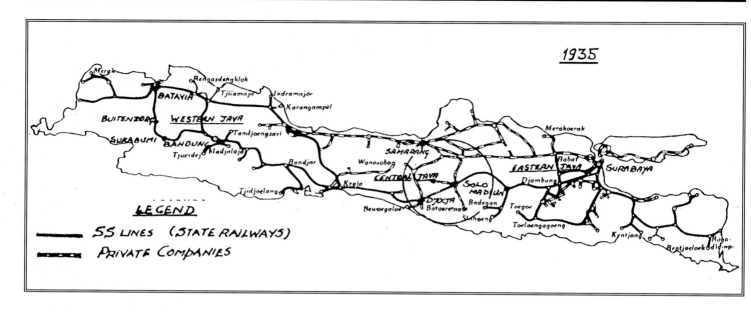

The writer would now like to describe in more general terms the State Railways (S.S.) system, which came into being in 1875 after protracted deliberations in both Houses of the Dutch Parliament in the 19th Century. There was a vociferous group of Parliamentarians who suggested the development of a road network on the island of Java (did we not hear that before), and to establish relay stations along the routes stocked with draught animals without , in the author's opinion, taking more cognisance of the fact that these animals would be prone to epidemical diseases, such as the rinder-pest, which could wipe out the entire stock in a short time, bringing all animal hauled transport to a standstill. This happened with the animal transportation system between South Africa and the newly opened up land of Rhodesia at the close of the last century, when the rinder pest created havoc and caused the system between the two countries to collapse. However, common sense prevailed and the first railway line in the 3'6" gauge was laid between Surabaya and Pasuruan, a distance of 63 km, inaugurated on 16th May 1878.

The 3'6" gauge, in Dutch called 'Kaaps Spoor' (Cape Gauge), was chosen by a commission specially set up to decide on the rail gauge for future railways. A battle of the gauges was waged in Parliament between the commission and the proponents of the 'broad gauge', who were another group of Parliamentarians mainly formed by the Directors of the now well established 4'8½" (1435 mm) gauge N.I.S. The decision was made to proceed in future with the 3'6" gauge for all new railways and so the largest railnet in that gauge was born in the Indonesian Archipelago. Whether the choice was right the author cannot say, but looking at the South African Railways of the same gauge, locomotive sizes approached those of the American steam locomotives built to far more generous proportions, and in the East Indies the locomotive sizes in many cases exceeded those of established locomotives in Europe. What they lacked in height they gained in girth, however, the writer is of the firm opinion that if mountainous and export orientated South Africa had adopted the 'standard' 4'8½" gauge, Southern Africa would have seen American sized steam locomotives on its metals.

Former Batavia Ooster Spoorweg 2-4-0T no. 6, one of three locos built by Beyer Peacock 1873/74. Photo: author's collection.

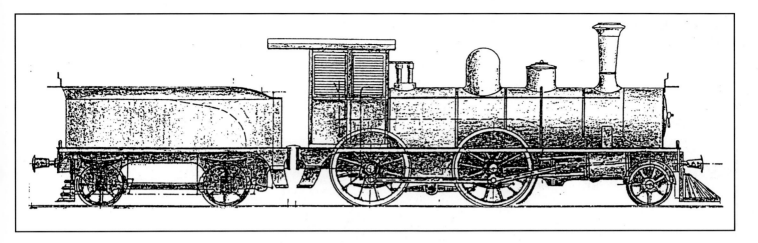

The Sharp Stewart 2-4-0 type as seen at Djèbrès shed in 1939 with an extended smokebox.

Early Staats Spoorwegen days with wood fired 2-4-0 locomotives. Photo: author's collection.

The first State Railway's locomotives were of diminutive size and of the tank type. It was mentioned elsewhere that the State took over the N.I.S. 3'6" gauge lines around the capital of Batavia, called the 'Batavia Ooster Spoorweg' or B.O.S. (Batavia Easter Railway) towards the close of the 19th Century and their no. 6 built by Beyer Peacock (illustrated) represents the size of locomotives during the formative years of the S.S.

A decade late in 1880 some larger passenger tender locomotives with 4-wheeled tenders were introduced, constructed by Sharp Stewart in Glasgow, Scotland. In the formative years the S.S. used wood fuel for their locomotives and this class of 2-4-0

tender locomotives was therefore provided with spark arresters and they were delivered as such. When the S.S. later on used coal fuel these engines lost their spark arresters. These locomotives had a long life extending into the 1970s and were well photographed.

In the closing years of the thirties decade with the Great Depression abating, the author observed two of these 2-4-0s stored at Djèbrès loco shed right up to 1939, the year of my departure. They must have been brought back into service afterwards or during the Japanese occupation. The two stored examples had extended smokeboxes as at an earlier date theses locomotives

Wood fired 2-4-0 B5012 built by Sharp Stewart in 1884 (works no. 3195), still working at Madiun on 13th April 1982.

Photo: Keith R. Chester.

Former Staats Spoorwegen no. 80 was seen on 26th January 1972 at Ponogoro having been converted to oil firing and renumbered to B5004. The loco has also been given a sand box and carries a re-railing jack on the running plate, no doubt an essential item!

Photo: D. Trevor Rowe.

were fitted with experimental superheaters manufactured by Werkspoor, however, only a few locomotives were so fitted, presumably the gains in boiler performance did not warrant the expense of the conversion and the remaining members of the class remained as saturated steam locos. They had two outside cylinders with inside D-valves and Stephenson valve motion.

At the close of the 19th Century the S.S. joined the prevailing fashion of compounding, especially with regard to the two-cylinder compound type. The leading proponent at the time was the German locomotive engineer von Borries, and his counterparts, the Englishman Worsdell and the Austrian Dr. Gölsdorf. Thus came into being the two-cylinder 4-4-0 compound tender locomotives of the 600 series, based on the 2c/4-4-0 express locomotives of the then Prussian State Railways. Being one of the author's favourite S.S. locomotives, many a time these two-cylin-

dered compounds were observed shunting in Solo-Balapan Yard. In their declining years they were assigned to the Kertosono - Blitar line with special crews because they were compounds. The writer had the satisfaction of once being hauled by one of these compounds on this line. The outside high pressure cylinder sat on the right hand side of the locomotive and the low pressure cylinder on the left, driven by Walschaert motion. They had a 'Lindner' starting valve.

The saturated compound steam locomotive became very popular in eastern Europe around the 1880-1900 period, especially in Austria, but also in the USA, where they were nicknamed 'slampounds'. As mentioned earlier, the S.S. in the early years of its existence and to a lesser extent the N.I.S. also joined the fashion, the two railways having between them the following two-cylinder compound locomotives at one time or another.

S.S. 3'6" (1067 mm) Gauge

Two-cylinder (outside) 0-6-0 compound tank locomotive,
      introduced 1892/1898   72 engines

Two-cylinder (outside) 2-6-0 compound tank locomotive,
      introduced 1892   83engines

Two-cylinder (outside) 4-4-0 compound tender locomotive,
      introduced 1900   54 engines

N.I.S. 3'6" (1067 mm) Gauge

Two-cylinder (inside) 0-4-2 compound tram tank locomotive,
      introduced 1898/1901   24 engines

N.I.S. 4'8½" (1435 mm) Gauge

Two-cylinder (outside) 4-6-0 compound tender locomotive,
      introduced 1902   6 engines

Two-cylinder (inside) 0-4-2 compound tender locomotive,
      reconstructed 1893/1901   11 engines

Early S.S. days with two cylinder compound 4-4-0 locomotives.
Photo: author's collection.

The 'honeymoon' with two-cylinder compounding came to an end round about the end of the first decade of the 20th Century with the introduction of the superheater and no further compound locomotives were built for the East Indies. In the light of the foregoing, with the considerable number of two-cylinder compounds running on the Javan railways, the author would lime to expound a little bit further on the subject of two-cylinder compounding.

The special advantage of the two-cylinder type of compound locomotive was its simplicity. Disadvantages, however, were the immense size necessary for the low pressure cylinder, the maximum permissible low pressure cylinder diameter was too limited, the difficulty of the total crank-pin pressure on the two sides alike, and the cost of the starting device. Re-admission of exhaust steam is also a problem. The high pressure cylinder cannot exhaust later than nine-tenths of its stroke, nor can the low pressure cylinder cut-off be earlier than three-tenths of its stroke. There are three pressures in the cylinders of a two-cylinder 'cross-compound',

namely the working (admission) pressure of the high-pressure cylinder, the exhaust pressure of the h.p. cylinder, which is practically equal to the working (admission) pressure of the low pressure cylinder, and the exhaust pressure of the low pressure cylinder.

From half to one rotation takes place before the high pressure exhausts opens the intercepting valve and closes the starting valve. As regards the starting power when boiler pressure steam is let into the receiver by the starting valve and the intercepting valve is thereby closed, the high pressure piston starts out against pressure in the receiver, which varies with the time that the engine has been standing. If the crank starts at 'dead point' on the high pressure side, the engine moves ¾ of a rotation before it commences to work as a compound. If the high pressure piston is near 'cut off' point on starting up, compound working will commence usually after approximately seven sixteenths of a rotation, depending on the position of the intercepting valve. If the crank on the high pressure side is in the position where the admission is cut off, the starting will be done by the low pressure cylinder alone, at least until the piston has reached a dead point, and

the engine works compound for about seven sixteenths of a rotation. So compared with simple engines having cylinders of the same area as the high pressure cylinder of the compound, the starting power of the compound will be greater, diminishing afterwards until it is about 80% to 85% of that of the two-cylinder simple engine.

The first successful two-cylinder compound locomotive was introduced in 1876 by the French Railway engineer Anatole Mallet of 'Mallet' locomotive fame for the Bayonne - Biarritz Railway in France, the same Bayonne where that horror piece of military hardware, the 'Bajonet' was invented in the 17th Century. This locomotive claimed a 25% fuel saving over a simple expansion saturated steam locomotive. As mentioned before, the great protagonist of two-cylinder compounding was the German locomotive engineer von Borries, who's first attempt was a tank locomotive of 1880 of the 2-2-0 wheel arrangement. Over the years the two-cylinder compound grew steadily in size, culminating in the huge USA Delaware & Hudson Railway two-cylinder compound high pressure locomotive of 1924 with a monstrous low pressure cylinder bore of 3'11½" (902 mm).

The classic two cylinder compound 4-4-0, built by Hartmann in 1905, was a scaled-down Saxon State Railways engine.
These two views of B5124 at Djakarta tanah Abang show the right hand high pressure cylinder (top),
and the large low pressure cylinder on the left hand side, (above). Photos: A.E. Durrant.

Former Staats Spoorwegen series 400 two cylinder compound 2-6-0T no. C1206, built by Hartmann in 1895, seen on the low pressure side in 1970. Photo: A.E. Durrant.

A steeply graded section of the line between Ambarawa and Setjang was provided with a rack, Java's only rack railway. 0-4-2 rack and adhesion locomotives built by Esslingen of Germany were used on this line. They were four-cylinder compounds, all four cylinders having the same bore. On level track only the pair of cylinders driving the adhesion wheels were used and when on the rack the other pair of cylinders cut in driving the rack gear, but then at double the revolutions of the adhesion drive. Sadly this rack railway is now out of normal revenue earning use, though it has been restored for tourism purposes, and the locos operating it are kept at Ambarawa's Railway Museum.

On account of the mixed gauge Jogjakarta's steam shed could cater for the 'broad gauge' as well as the 'standard gauge'. The N.I.S. also ran a 3'6" gauge line between the capital of Batavia (Jakarta) and Buitenzorg conceived in the latter part of the 19th century, but this line was taken over by the state long before the author's time. In addition, the N.I.S. also possessed a 3'6" gauge railway connecting the port cities of Samarang and Surabaya. This line was part of the through connection along Java's north coast between the cities of Batavia and Surabaya mentioned in an earlier chapter. It was, however, a secondary line and passengers had to break their journey to change trains. Today it is a through

connection without a break of journey and is preferred over the old line via Jogjakarta, Solo and Madiun due to its shorter distance.

The N.I.S. used 4-6-0 tender locomotives built by the Manchester firm of Beyer Peacock in Britain on this route for their express passenger trains. They had Belpaire boilers and were superheated. In 1937 the administration seriously contemplated introducing diesel multiple units between Samarang and Surabaya and had a couple of train sets built by Beynes of Haarlem in Holland (the author's home town). This name in the Dutch railway industry and their assembly halls were situated opposite the imposing railway station of Haarlem. Today this enterprise is no more and where once the large premises stood is now a busy bus terminal and 'plaza'. Nothing remains any more as a reminder of the past railway activities. However, the war intervened and the train sets never arrived in the East Indies. They were lying in Haarlem railway yard during the war years, rusting away, as the writer could observe, standing on Haarlem station platform.

As the N.I.S. steam shops were situated in Jogjakarta, at the time catering for both standard and broad gauges and lacking a 3'6" gauge connection between Samarang and Jogjakarta (which

Rack and adhesion compound 0-4-2T B2502 at Djakarta in 1970. The works plate reads No. 3244 Maschinen Fabrik Esslingen Emil Kessler 1902. Photo: A.E. Durrant.

materialised via Solo in 1940 by laying a 3rd rail), any 3'6" gauge rolling stock from the Samarang-Surabaya line needing repairs or attention were transported over the 'broad gauge' on multi-axled transporter wagons. Many a time the author observed these vehicles coming through Solo carrying a steam locomotive.

Below: One of the former N.I.S. 3'6" gauge 4-6-0s built by Beyer Peacock, C5107. Photo: Keith R. Chester.

Three gauges at a point between Solo and Djocjakarta. On the left is the 3'6" gauge S.S. main line laid in 1928/29, on the right is the N.I.S. 4'8½" gauge main line of 1899, with a 3rd rail for N.I.S. 3'6" gauge traffic, and crossing over both is a 600 mm gauge sugar cane railway.

The narrow gauge crossover is of a type known as a 'Hobbel Kruising' (bumpy crossing), not permitted to be used by locomotives - see also the diagram on page 63.

Photo: author's collection.

The Parade of Staats Spoorwegen Locomotives at Solo Junction

Solo Junction was a veritable steam paradise and the variety of locomotive types was bewildering, with the N.I.S. 4'8½" 'broad gauge' having a sizeable locomotive shed with fuel depot and turntable, the 3'6" gauge tramway system having a steam depot at Purwosari Station, and the standard 3'6" gauge S.S. having a medium sized shed at Djèbrès Station, also with fuel depot and turntable.

The S.S. was very much a railway of round topped wide fireboxes with 'Coale' safety valves, except for some elderly locomotives and in many respects followed American practice in contrast to the Netherland Indies Railway which had more of a British look. Excepting the American built 2-8-8-0 mallet locomotives provided with 'Mellin' steam reversing gear and some elderly locomotives fitted with Johnson Bar reversing gear, reversing was done with the screw reverser. The majority of locomotives had two boiler feedwater steam injectors but a goodly number of the larger locomotives were provided with feedwater apparatus of some sort or another. Except for the elderly locomotives fitted with Allan valve gear and the occasional Stephenson valve gear, all locomotives were fitted with Walschaert motion and were superheated and, apart from the American Mallets, all locomotives followed the German practice of having piston tail-rods. Crosshead guides were of the 'Alligator' type and bogie tenders ran on American type 'diamond' bogies. The more modern locomotives all carried mechanical lubricators. The series 300 two cylinder 2-6-0 simple expansion tank locomotives and the series 400 two-cylinder 2-6-0 compound tank locomotives of identical construction and totalling 131 engines all had Allan valve gear.

The steam whistle varied from one locomotive class to another, with the big S.S. Mallets and most of the freight engines having a chime whistle and the passenger locomotives having a 'Dutch shriek' whistle. At the N.I.S. the passenger tram locomotives had the more mellow 'Saxon' single tone whistle, whilst the heavy 'Consolidations' either had a chime whistle or a 'Stanier hooter'. Sitting quietly at home with the 'house' in earshot from the yards, one could pretty well follow the comings and goings of that railway company.

The S.S. over the years developed its own styling of locomotives with lipped chimneys and conical smokebox doors, but after

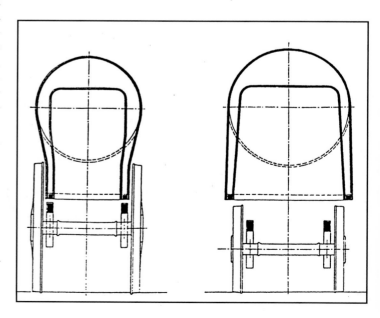

S.S. round top narrow and wide firebox diagrams.

the newer locomotives underwent front-end improvements in the early and mid 1930s the lipped chimney in many cases made way for the stove-pipe chimney, which in the opinion of the writer did not always improve the looks of the engines so treated. The thirties was also the time that smoke deflectors of the German type appeared on some locomotives. This presumably went hand in hand with the exhaust improvements that gave a less fierce blast. The author is not aware of any front end improvements carried out on N.I.S. locomotives, their latest 4-6-0 express locomotives having Kylala blastpipe arrangements anyway. The 'broad gauge' locomotives never carried smoke deflectors but their 3'6" gauge 4-6-0 express locos did. Duplex exhausts were fitted only on the big Mallets. Kylchaps, Giesels and Lempors were either a novelty or decades away. The American type of cowcatcher was introduced on the S.S. late in the 19th Century after a train on the Batavia - Tandjung Priok line derailed at speed with great loss of life after hitting a stray water buffalo.

All the 'broad gauge' and 3'6" gauge tram locomotives were wood fired, the wood originating from the extensive teak forests of Eastern Java. The SS locomotives were fired with a low grade bituminous coal imported

The S.S. 3'6" gauge class 300 simple expansion 2-6-0T (upper) and the class 400 compound version (lower). Drgs: J.R.

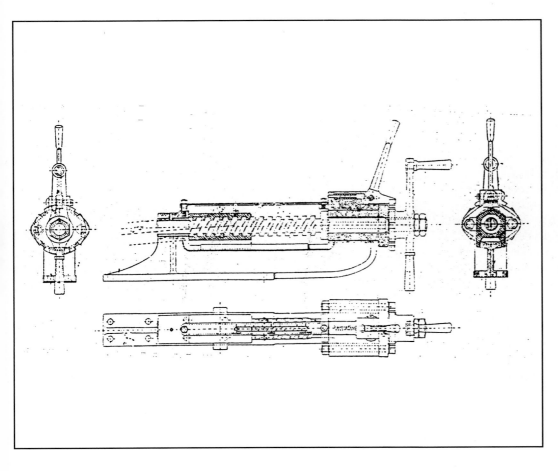

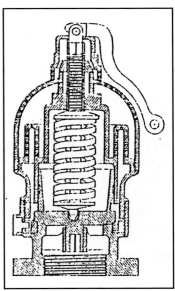

'Coale' safety valve

Left: Working diagram of a screw reverser

S.S. 4-4-0 no. 660 makes an interesting comparison with the Borsig 4-4-0s, being a two cylinder simple expansion engine built by Werkspoor (354/1914). In later days this loco became PNKA B5310. Works photo courtesy of Ian G.T. Duncan.

Staats Spoorwegen 2-6-2T no. 1771 was another Werkspoor product, works no. 601 of 1929, renumbered later on to C3071.
Works photo courtesy of Ian G.T. Duncan.

Below: 2-8-0 no. 920 was one of the batch supplied by SLM, Winterthur, but indistinguishable from the Dutch built members of the class.
Photo: author's collection, courtesy of SLM.

from state owned coal mines in Central Sumatra and shipped out to the Javan state railways. The island of Java did not have coal deposits but had extensive oilfields at Tjepu (Cepu), near Central Java's north coast. At an early stage oil firing was tried in conjunction with coal firing but apparently the copper fireboxes did not take too kindly to this type of petroleum residue fuel and no further attempts were made till after World War II, when the Indonesian State Railways successfully and extensively used oil firing after presumably steel fireboxes were introduced during major overhauls (1955). Probably the Japanese occupation during the war years had a hand in the introduction of steel fireboxes on the Javan railways, but the writer cannot say for sure.

In its formative years the S.S. had also used wood fuel extensively but went over to coal firing. The large Mallets used a mixture of coal and coal briquettes, the briquettes being produced out of coal fines and pitch at a state own0 facility at Tandjung-

Mixed solid and liquid fuel firing was adopted for some classes of loco, such as the standard gauge N.I.S. 2-6-2T seen here at Willem I (now better known as Ambarawa). This system of firing was well known to the author at Solo. Picture postcard view courtesy of C.J. Walker

Hulpstation Willem I.

Priok. The Indonesian State Railways after World War II still used wood fuel on a considerable scale. The Sumatran low grade bituminous coal, more of kind of Lignite, could not be kept for long in the open (three months), before oxidation set in and could not be stored and heaped higher than between one and two metres. Therefore the coal fuel depot at Djèbrès shed at the time observed consisted of a palisade of old sleepers with coal heaped one metre high within and the locomotives were fueled by hand using baskets.

The Javan 4'8½" 'broad gauge' went into oblivion during the War years as the Japanese occupation saw fit to dismantle Java's oldest railway, the materials to 'exported' to other war zones.

The Djèbrès locomotive facility was a three road medium sized shed, the like of which could be commonly found in the smaller centres, the larger centres having more extensive facilities. Solo-Djèbrès was a much smaller centre with engines just lying over, although it must have seen better days when the rails westwards stopped at Solo in times gone by. Madiun, further to the east, became the larger centre as the main steam workshops were established there. Having the main works in Madiun probably accounted for the variety of locomotive classes that could be observed in Solo, the stretch of line from Solo to Madiun being used to run out the final miles before shopping and to 'break in' newly outshopped locomotives, as the writer many a time observed a freshly painted, newly overhauled engine.

The author never caught sight of a steam breakdown crane. This equipment was presumably domiciled at the larger centres with 'shopping' facilities like Madiun (S.S.) and Jogjakarta (N.I.S.).

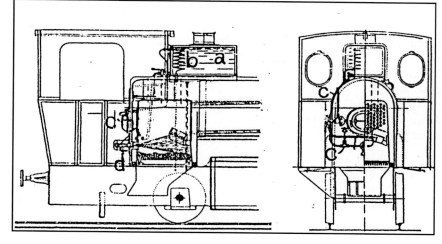

Firing system with mixed solid and liquid fuel.
a = fuel oil tank, b = steam heat coil, c = controls, d = burner.

Right: The Briquette Press.
Photo: author's coll.

25

Serious mishaps were never heard of but minor ones certainly occurred in the yards, such as 'splitting the points' where a locomotive might derail if the points had not been properly set. Turntables were predominantly of the 'armstrong' types (you need strong arms . . .), but the S.S. also used wyes or turning triangles. Solo Junction had two turntables, one S.S. and one

N.I.S. Locomotive water was provided from steel tanks, mostly placed on a brick structure, the water being pumped up from the nearby river (Balapan Yard) or from wells. Swing out water columns of the German type were used at S.S. as well as N.I.S. facilities. In Germany in the olden days these water columns were 'Baroque' styled, real examples of the foundryman's art.

Several pairs of strong arms are required if the locomotive to be turned is a class D52 2-8-2! D52097 is seen on Cikampek turntable on 1st July 1980, a Krupp built loco (3320/1951). Photo: Keith R. Chester.

Below: Both of these classes of Mallet were seen at Solo, though Dusty's photo shows them at Tjibatu, heading a mixed train to Tjitjalengka. The leading engine is a former S.S. 1600 class 2-6-6-0, running as PNKA CC5001, behind which is one of the class CC10 2-6-6-0T Mallets. Photo: A.E. Durrant.

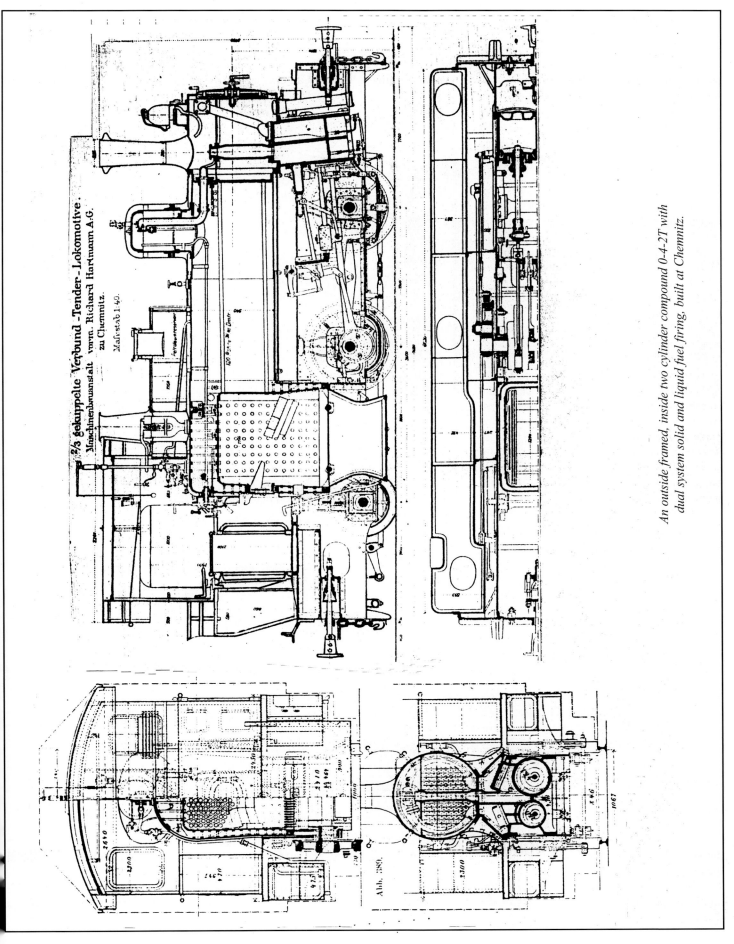

2/3 gekuppelte Verbund-Tender-Lokomotive.

Maschinenbauanstalt vorm. Richard Hartmann A.G.
zu Chemnitz.

Maßstab 1:40.

Abb. 389.

An outside framed, inside two cylinder compound 0-4-2T with dual system solid and liquid fuel firing, built at Chemnitz.

The Solo Tramway

Java's oldest railway ran a tramway from Bojolali via Solo to Baturetno. The trackage was invariably laid parallel to existing roads, as in Europe. Solo, or Surakarta, in the early days boasted a horse-drawn tram owned by the Solo Tramsweg Maatschappij (Solo Tramway Company), absorbed later by the Netherland-Indies Railway Company (N.I.S.) who extended the system and in the first two decades of the century ran tram trains pulled by (inside) two-cylindered 0-6-0 wood fired tank locomotives.

These tram trains were mostly composed of the locomotive and auxiliary tender or water cart, followed by a couple of bogie stock economy class passenger coaches with hard seating, with a couple of 'standard gauge' (3'6") goods wagons bringing up the rear. These economy class coaches had longitudinally placed bench seating as of course a fair amount of livestock also travelled inside. They had open verandahs with the handbrake in easy reach. The crew consisted of driver, fireman, brakeman and the white-capped conductor. Speed was modest at 25 km per hour. On its travels through the city the tram could pick up passengers at several wayside halts consisting of a short crossing spur worked by spring loaded points, to let opposing trams pass. It was always a joy to behold to see a tram train puffing through town with the bell clanging incessantly and whistling for every street crossing. In those far off days

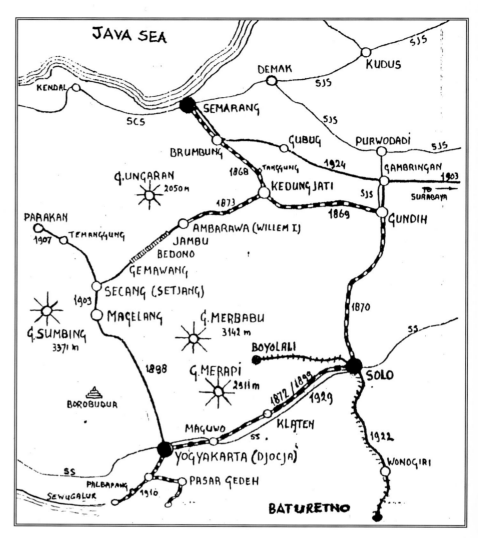

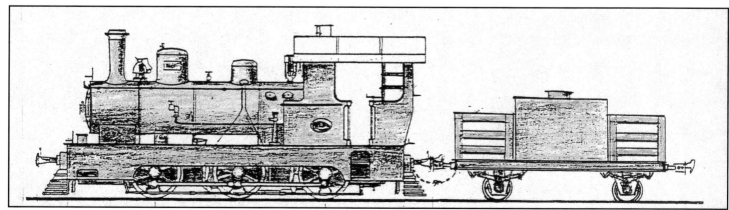

0-6-0 Tram locomotive with auxiliary tender. Drg. J.R.

the street traffic consisted mainly of horse-drawn carriages and the occasional car.

The 0-6-0 tank locomotives were neat little machines weighing in at 25 tons with Walscheart valve motion built by the Chemnitz works of the Saxon Locomotive Works, formerly

Richard Hartmann of Germany. They carried a regulation steam worked bell on the boiler front and were provided with an auxiliary tender or water cart constructed out of a four-wheeled vehicle chassis, with a square or rectangular water tank in the centre and a crate at each end for the firewood. The water connection to the locomotive was via a rubber hose. The tram train was hand braked but the locomotive was provided with a steam brake and a handbrake. Drawbar gear was of the East Indies 'standard gauge' "Pihl" system, with safety chains also used by the S.S. In the opinion of the writer, these self-couplers, like the American 'buckeye' coupler were the greatest invention after the steam locomotive, dramatically reducing the serious injuries sometimes sustained when coupling up.

There was a small tram loco depot at Purwosari station with

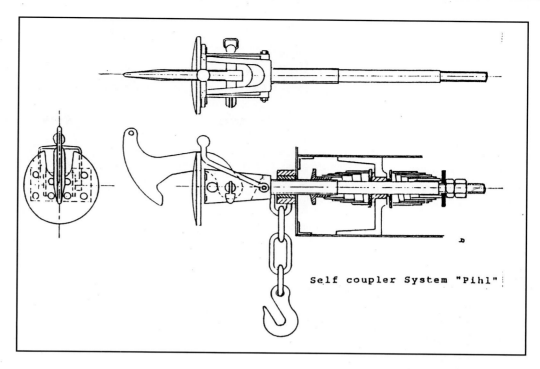

Right: The 'Pihl' self coupler.

watering facilities consisting of a water tank and a well. Many times, a tram locomotive on shed could be observed pumping water from the well into the storage tank using a steam pump placed at well level with the loco under steam providing the driving force. This setup presumably dated back to the early days before the town had electricity.

These tram locos also frequented Solo's main station, Balapan, to deliver or pick up goods wagons only. The 3'6" state railway's section of this station had one platform frequented by the 3'6" gauge N.I.S. trains, these trains having access to the station yard via a 3rd rail laid in the 4'8½" 'broad gauge' track between Purwosari station and Balapan station. As a matter of

fact this 3rd rail extended right from Solo to Jogjakarta, laid in 1899 to enable the State Railways to bridge the gap between the two towns as they had no connecting track of their own until 1929.

The N.I.S. ran 3'6" gauge trains via this 3rd rail connection to Jogjakarta and to the towns of Magelang and Ambarawa. On these trains a larger type of two-cylindered superheated 2-6-2 wood fired tank locomotive with Belpaire boiler was used, designed and built by Werkspoor of Amsterdam. These tank locomotives were fitted with vacuum brakes as they ran on the main line. The rack line between Ambarawa and Setjang was described in the chapter about the 3'6" gauge railway system.

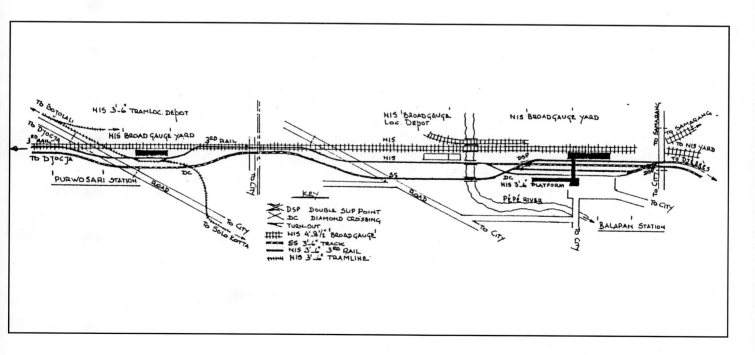

The 3rd rail connection between Purwosari and Balapan stations. Drg. J.R.

Tramway Views in Batavia and Surabaya

Right: Meester Cornelis tramway terminus in Batavia's suburbs with an 0-4-0 fireless tram loco built by Hohenzollern in 1889.
Postcard view courtesy of Christopher Walker.

The Nederlands-Indische Tramweg Maatshappij operated the street railway in Batavia. Fireless 0-4-0 tram loco no. 26 stands with a flat wagon and three carriages at an attractive shelter with staff posing for the picture. The loco is one of the original Hohenzollerns built 1882-1909 and originally numbered 1-21.
Postcard view courtesy of Christopher Walker.

At the eastern end of the country, two Surabaja system steam trams were seen at Wonokromo in January 1972. B1242 is a Beyer Peacock product of 1905 but its companion, B1245, was built at the Semerang Works in 1923.
Photo: D. Trevor Rowe.

The Vanished Railway (4'8½", 1435 mm 'Broad' Gauge)

In preceding chapters mention was made of the 4'8½" 'Broad Gauge' railway owned and operated by the Netherland Indies Railway Company (N.I.S.), which ran the line from the port of Samarang on Java's north coast to Jogjakarta via Solo, with branch lines to Ambarawa and to the sugar cane growing area south of Jogjakarta. The first track was laid in 1864 and the first trains ran in 1867 on a 25 km stretch, with further stretches of track opened up in the following years (see dates on the map on page 28). The total demise came in the early Forties when the Japanese Military Occupation forces dismantled the 4'8½" gauge railway to be transported to Manchuria (Manchukwo).

During its formative years this railway was very much a 'Beyer-Peacock' railway, this Manchester firm of locomotive builders supplying most of the locomotives, which were of the inside 2-cylindered unsuperheated tender type and very 'Stroudley' looking. Later on the Administration turned to German and Dutch locomotive builders, such as the Saxon Locomotive and Machine works, formerly Richard Hartmann of Chemnitz in German Saxony, and the engineering works of Werkspoor in Amsterdam. The author had the satisfaction of seeing early examples of at least two of the aforementioned locomotive builders, with a goodly number of the Beyer-Peacock 'shade of Stroudley' locomotives still in daily service and with some of the early Werkspoor inside cylindered 2-6-2 tank locomotives stored away in a dark corner of Solo's 'broad gauge' steam shed at Solo-Balapan, which locos had not turned a wheel

'Broad' gauge 0-4-2 no. 29 at Solo Balapan station heading a passenger train some time in the 1930s.
Photographer unknown,
Courtesy of Christopher Walker.

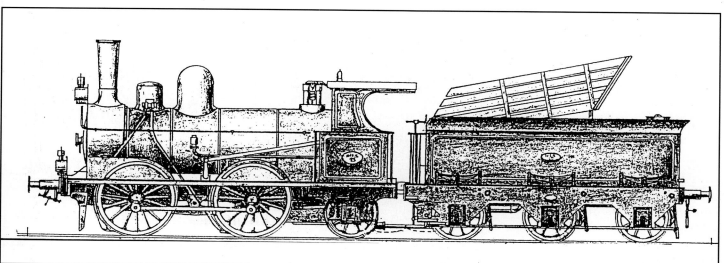

Beyer Peacock 0-4-2 inside 2-cylinder compound passenger locomotive. Drg. J.R.

in years, being poor performers.

The Administration further owned outside 2-cylindered unsuperheated shunting engines with inside mounted Stephenson valve gear and several series of outside 2-cylindered unsuperheated and superheated 4-6-0 passenger tender locomotives. A series of outside 2-cylindered superheated 2-8-0 'Consolidation' type of freight tender locomotives added to the bewildering array of 'broad gauge' and 'standard gauge' locos to be observed at Solo Junction. All the 'broad gauge' locomotives burned wood fuel, although in the formative years coal had been used.

The N.I.S. railway was very much a company of Belpaire narrow firebox boilers and Ramsbottom safety valves, in contrast to the State Railways which predominantly used round-top wide fireboxes with Coale safety valves, except for a few oldtimers. All locomotives except for the 0-4-2s and the 0-6-0 shunting engines and a few elderly 4-6-0s carried electric lighting. All 'broad gauge' locomotives were fitted with Hardy vacuum brakes except for shunting engines which braked on the steam brake and handbrake. The 0-4-2 and 0-6-0 locomotives had Johnson bar reversers but newer locomotives were fitted with screw reversers. The series 121 express locomotives carried a Knorr type feedwater heater and were fitted with Kylala blastpipes, giving the exhaust

beat a peculiar whistling sound. All N.I.S. locomotives were painted black with polished boiler bands and red buffer beams, but the top-link engines of the 121 series changed to a sort of olive green lined out in red when the Depression abated towards the end of the Thirties, at which time the railways started to rejuvenate their rolling stock and improved on train timings.

The first trains were pulled by the 0-4-2 tender locomotives constructed by Beyer-Peacock which evolved into the final type of wood-fired 2-cylinder compounds. These 0-4-2s originally had two high pressure cylinders but were compounded before and during the turn of the last century, as was the vogue in those days, and the conversion was so successful that the Administration decided to convert the entire class bar a few engines, with the new cylinder blocks presumably supplied by Beyer Peacock. A later series of these economical locomotives were aptly named 'Hardlopers' (Fast Runners), on account of their speed capabilities. They had round-top fireboxes for a change and were fitted with Ramsbottom safety valves.

Many a time the author observed them waddling past at speed on a mixed train with the measured beat so characteristic of a two cylinder compound. The writer also observed them on the 'Shunt' at Solo-Balapan and Purwosari yards, with the engine's starting

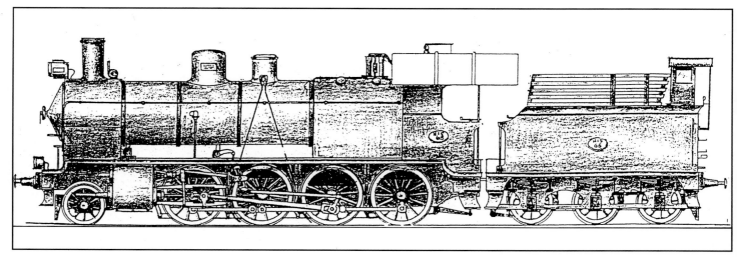

Top: Hartmann 4-6-0 two cylinder simple expansion passenger locomotive, series 89-94.
Above: Hartmann 2-8-0 'Consolidation' goods locomotive, series 61-68. Drgs: J.R.

performance interesting to watch, moving a goodly turn of the wheels before the first exhaust beat. They were fitted with vacuum brakes and steam brake on the engine and a handbrake on the tender. Noticeable was the large 'crate' fitted on the tender to store the firewood. Being built to the English loading gauge at the time, the other locomotives built to the larger European continental loading gauge towered over these locomotives.

Generally the 2-axled freight rolling stock lacked vacuum brakes but some goods wagons had handbrakes fitted which operated from roof level. For that reason a brakesman's seat was fitted at roof level with a number of 'Brakies' strewn out over the length of the goods train when in motion, all acting on signals given on the locomotive whistle. Many a time the writer clambered up on a wagon to have a glorious overview, but could imagine that the 'Brakie' of course would take a dimmer view of that vista, perched high up on the moving train when hit by a tropical downpour during the wet Monsoon. Some goods wagons of later construction had 'Doghouses' fitted for the brakesman like on the European continental railways, which improved conditions very much during inclement weather.

The predominant freight rolling stock of the 2-axled version would be the enclosed sugar wagon and molasses tank car, as this railway in its heyday transported countless bags of sugar to the ports. Other rolling stock counted a lesser number of 2-axled petrol tankers and bogie flatcars for long timbers, logs, rails, and constructional steel, as well as livestock wagons, mostly used for the transportation of the wood fuel to supply depots along the line. Special vehicles were the multi-axled rolling stock transporter wagons mentioned in an earlier chapter and the Funeral Car, of which more later. The author never caught sight of the steam breakdown crane and fitted goods trains were never observed.

Passenger bogie stock was of the corridor type, ran on the English type of bogie, and had 1st. 2nd and 3rd class compart-

ments. The 4th class passengers were hard-seated in 2-axled vehicles with a veranda on each end. They provided reasonably comfortable cheap travel for the masses. Overloaded passenger trains like we sometimes see on motion pictures of the Indian Railways were unknown at that time on the Javan Railways. Everyone was seated. Draw and buffing gear was of the European type of screw coupling with safety chains added. The main line trains had bogie luggage vans or baggage cars as they were called, being the first vehicle behind the locomotive, with facilities to carry a doggie, or even a larger animal for that matter. Doggies had to travel in the baggage car. On 'mixed' trains probably occasionally a goat or other domestic animal travelled in the 2-axled 4th class coach. Being fitted with a vacuum brake these vehicles were arranged directly behind the locomotive as the goods rolling stock was not 'fitted'. Some locomotives had a bell mounted on the tender or against the cab roof with a cord strung from the locomotive along the side of the coaches enabling the conductor to signal the driver to stop at a halt for passengers to be picked up or dropped off by pulling the cord, all gadgets long since disappeared from the railway scene.

The writer proceeded once to Jogjakarta by train with other classmates for an aural school examination and when returning the train had one of these 0-4-2s on the head end. We were making good time, followed in the distance by the S.S. 'Day Express', Solo bound on the adjacent 3'6" (1067 mm) gauge track doing at least 90-100 km/h, trying to overtake before the next station. The bet was on, but the big Pacific won the day and during the remainder of the month one had to do without pocket money. The footplate of the 0-4-2 must have been rather 'lively', the engine falling over its own feet trying to keep pace with Big Brother. When the Pacific glided past at arm's length with thundering exhaust, one could observe for a while from out of the train window the goings-on on its footplate.

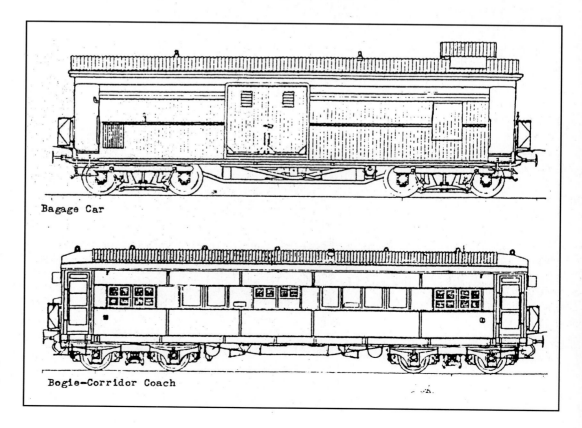

The standard N.I.S. 4'8½" broad gauge baggage car and bogie corridor coach.

Bagage Car

Bogie-Corridor Coach

In 1902 the first 4-6-0 tender locomotives were ordered by the N.I.S. from the Saxon Locomotive Works (formerly Richard Hartmann) in Chemnitz, in eastern Germany. They were two cylinder compounds with 6-wheeled tenders dictated by the length of the then available turntables. They were copies of the Norwegian State Railways 4-6-0 2-cylinder compound locomotives with bogie tenders, also built by the Saxon Locomotive Works. These first ten-wheelers had D-valves driven by Walschearts gear. They were modernised during the Twenties but with the introduction of the more modern series 121-124 two cylinder simple expansion 4-6-0s of 1923 these compounds went into storage. The maximum speed of the series 121-124 was set at 90 km/h but at the end of the Thirties with the general speeding up of train timings the Administration was looking around for additional express locomotives and enquired at the Netherland Railways if they were prepared to release a few of their highly successful class 3700 4-cylinder 4-6-0 express locomotives, however, the NS (Netherland Railways) had none to spare but offered other 4-6-0s. The N.I.S. declined the offer and asked

Werkspoor for a quotation for new locomotives. At that time the streamlining of steam locomotives was in vogue and the proposed engines would not be an exception, however, the ensuing European War put paid to the intentions. Nos. 121, 122, and 123 carried names, respectively 'W. Poolman', 'G.C. Daum', and 'J.P. de Bordes'. J.P. de Bordes was the construction engineer of the line in 1864.

There is now no trace left of this railway except for the Right of Way now occupied by 3'6" track and an occasional rusting hulk in some railway backyard, as the Japanese Occupation saw fit to dismantle Java's oldest railway in its entirety, intending to transport the materials and rolling stock to Manchuria, which they only partly managed. An inglorious end to such a once thriving system. How the Manchu crews were supposed to cope with the harsh northern Chinese winters in the open 'tropical' locomotive cabs is anybody's guess, but then the Japanese Imperial High Command was not given over to sentimentality. With 'Glasnost' now extending to the Chinese mainland may be someone one day will write a treatise on the Manchurian Railways during the

SIX COUPLED COMPOUND PASSENGER LOCOMOTIVE, INDIAN NETHERLANDS RAILWAY (JAVA). 567.

Netherland Indies Railway 4'8½" gauge compound 4-6-0 no. 82, built by Hartmann (2768/1902), one of the locomotives that disappeared during the Second World War, probably transported to Manchuria.
Postcard view courtesy of Christopher Walker.

N.I.S. goods locomotive no. 64, a two-cylinder simple expansion 2-8-0 also produced at the Hartmann factory (3541/1912). Leading dimensions are given on the opposite page.
Postcard view courtesy of Christopher Walker.

1-D Güterzugslokomotive der Niederländisch-Indischen Bahn.
Erbaut von der Sächs.-Masch.-Fabrik vorm. Rich. Hartmann in Chemnitz

Pacific War and we will come to know about the fate of some of the N.I.S. rolling stock, if it ever arrived at its destination. It is possible that some of this rolling stock is lying at the bottom of the Chinese Sea. Who knows? Also, a goodly number of 3'6" gauge S.S. 2-6-2 tank locomotives as well as the 3'6" gauge N.I.S. 4-6-0 tender locomotives were 'exported' by the Japanese Occupation during the Pacific War, predominantly to Laos and Cambodia.

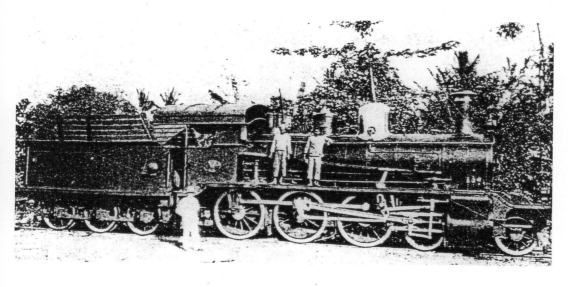

Working broad gauge steam. Hopefully the rarity of these two views from the author's collection makes up for their poor photographic quality.
Left: One of the 4-6-0 compounds of 1902, with added tender capacity.
Below: An 0-4-2 compound working tender first on a mixed train. The exposed seat for the 'Brakie' is just discernable on the roof of the leading goods van

Leading Dimensions of the N.I.S. 4'8½" Gauge 2-8-0s

Cylinder Diameter	540 mm	Heating surface	205.5 sq.m
Piston Stroke	650 mm	Weight Empty	59,500 kg
Driving Wheel dia.	1,445 mm	Weight in Working Order	66,000 kg
Grate area	2.58 sq.m	Maximum Permitted Speed	60 km/hour

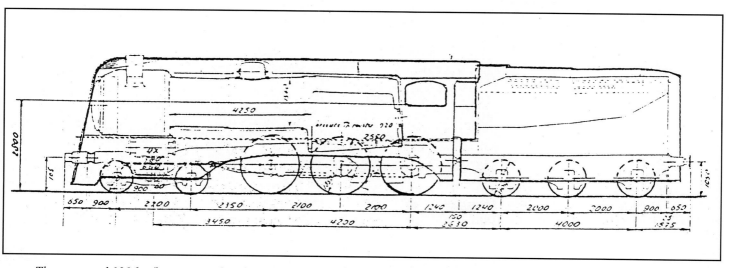

The proposed 120 km/hour streamlined N.I.S. two cylinder 4-6-0 express locomotive. Drg: Werkspoor, author's collection.

Shed Bashing!

The author would like to comment on the aspects of pre-war East Indies shed-bashing (over 60 years ago), which in his case was always a one-man affair. The hordes of shed-bashers as known in England in steam days, trying to penetrate the holiest of holies, were unknown in the Indies at that time. Therefore, easy access to the railway installations could be had, mainly due to the fact that one was a 'Sinjo' (European lad), and there were not many of those around at the time, and because one was a lone specimen of the shed-bashing breed. As a matter of fact, the writer in nine years of shed-bashing never ever met a fellow specimen. In most cases, ignoring at one's own peril the 3 gradations of 'no trespassing' warning notices such as 'No Entry', 'Strictly No Entry', or 'Strictly No Entry, article so and so of the Penal Code', one got easy access to the railway premises, which were not fenced off or walled. That would not have helped anyway as the locals on foot used the line of rail as the shortest distance between A and B, and that included the yards.

Access to the premises was therefore unhindered providing one kept oneself in the background, with access to the private railway company's installations somewhat easier than the State owned premises, which was understandable as is the case with state run enterprises. Of course there were uniformed railway guards around 'clocking' their territory but they totally ignored the 'Sinjo', probably thinking the lad was the son of some railway official. One of the classmates was the son of the District Civil Engineer and occasionally mentioning his name would open 'no-go' areas. One never saw high placed officialdom, or it had to be the local Stationmaster on his regular inspection tours of the premises urging one to be careful.

A favourite pastime during the author's shed-bashing was to hitch a ride on the front unit of a State Railways Mallet riding the turntable, but if one were per chance spotted by the Shedmaster, if he was around, a shout would follow out of the confines of the gloomy engine house urging one to 'Getoutofhere', not an unreasonable proposition as an amputation could be instantaneous. Having ridden the Mallet, which emanated great sighs from the cavernous low pressure cylinders, and been doused with oily and sooty condensate ejected from the slobbering chimney, one had to

Bashing the shed at Tjibatu in 1970 and 1971 'Dusty' Durrant found an allocation comprised solely of compound Mallets. Here lined up are 2-6-6-0 CC5002, 2-8-8-0 DD5208, and 2-6-6-0T CC1032, with their proud foreman.

The most popular class with Indonesian crews were the class 1300, later type C28, 4-6-4T.
C2813 on shed at Purwokerto depot on 11th July 1980 was constructed by Henschel (18167/1921). Photo: Keith R. Chester.

slink into the bathroom at home to avoid the wrath of Mama. The Head of the Family did not object to Sonnyboy's railway exploits so long as he behaved himself, went to Sunday School or Church on Sunday, and got satisfactory marks at school. This could be challenging as one found one's self in the company of an ethnic variety of classmates (discrimination went out of the window, promulgated by a 1909 law), the class in many instances being lectured by Papa himself and one was expected to be an example to the class.

Anyone at the railways given some authority was called a 'Chef', such as 'Stations Chef' (Stationmaster), or 'Chef Weg an Werken' (Chief Civil Engineer), or 'Chef Tractie en Materiel' (Chief Mechanical Engineer), but strangely enough the highest in the hierarchy of Chefs and Sous-Chefs was called the 'Hoofdinspecteur', freely translated as Chief Inspector or Chief Superintendent (General Manager). An acquaintance of the parents at the time, having been at the same school, was a travelling locomotive inspector with the State Railways, based at Madiun Workshops, who when doing his inspection tours always dropped in at the parental home for a cold beer. Invariably this person when visiting got pestered for photographs. The last the writer saw of him was in 1939, riding the footplate of a 1300 class 4-6-4 express tank locomotive pulling out of Balapan station heading for Madiun with a long goods train. He was never seen again, probably lost in the ensuing 'Pacific Holocaust'.

Stationmasters, shop foremen, top link drivers, drivers, firemen, conductors, yardmasters and lower administrative staff, in other words the rank-and-file, were 100% ethnic, with the Eurasian mostly finding a niche as engine driver, sub-shedmaster, or as Sous-Chef in the Civil Engineer's Department. The conduc-

tor in the East Indies, especially those on the crack expresses was a man of great importance and a respected member of his community who brooked no nonsense from high spirited scholars travelling from or to their respective boarding schools during vacations. The 'Tukangs' (artisans) in the sheds were always forthcoming when asked questions about their work and were good in their trade. Locomotives always looked spick and span with polished steel boiler bands and brass fittings and paintwork well maintained. The writer can remember practically never hearing a 'knock' or 'ringing rods', or it was to be near shopping time. A goodly number of locomotives carried boiler jackets from 'Russian iron' and displayed a beautiful bluish shine.

Climbing on the footplate of locomotives at rest or during a shunting pause and looking into the glow of the firebox, asking questions about the size of the firebox, invariably one got a prosaic answer such as "It cooks a sappi (ox) in one minute." The driver was called 'Masjinis' from the Dutch word 'machinist', and the fireman was called the 'Stoker', in contrast to the Netherlands where the driver was called 'Machinist' or 'Meester' and the fireman being the 'Learling' (pupil).

The N.I.S. sparingly named their engines, in total only three express engines, but the S.S. refrained from naming their locomotives altogether. Some classes must have had nicknames given to them by operating personnel but the writer only knows of the N.I.S. 0-4-2s being known as 'Hardlopers', as mentioned earlier, and the sizeable fleet of S.S. 2-6-0 tank locos, all built at the Richard Hartmann works, known as 'Chemnitzers'.

Locomotive design was in the hands of the 'Department van Koloniën' (State Department of the Colonies), in conjunction with the manufacturers, the State Department acting as a sort of

Crown Agent. The majority of designs were successful and had long lives, the Indonesian engineman's delight, pre-war as well as post-war, being the large 4-6-4T express tank engines of the pre-war series 1300, notwithstanding questions raised at the time as to the need of such an engine.

Werkspoor participated many times in the manufacture of Indonesian locomotive classes and the author notes with pride, the ability of one of the smallest locomotive manufacturing firms in Europe at that time to churn out for export large Mallets and large non-articulated steam locomotives of superb workmanship. Electric and diesel locomotives, and DMUs and EMUs were also built for export, as well as for the home market. Alas, this firm ceased manufacturing rolling stock a long time ago, being absorbed by other engineering enterprises, and ceased trading under the name of 'Werkspoor'.

Shortly after the war and before returning to work for plantations in Sumatra, the author found employment with Werkspoor in their 'Physics and Dynamics' department, mainly working on torsional vibration problems in marine diesel-driven ship propulsion systems, the head of this department having solved the problems of crankshaft fractures due to torsion vibrations of the diesel traction engines used on the Netherlands Railways' DMUs introduced during the mid-thirties for branch line services. This firm also built huge marine diesel engines of up to 30,000 hp and had a fitting out basin. Shortly after the War the firm did a considerable amount of refurbishment of war damaged steam locomotives and other rolling stock for Netherlands Railways. The writer's lunch hour was spent many times in the boiler shop and locomotive assembly halls observing the progress made with the refurbishments. The Indonesian State Railways after the War never returned to Werkspoor for further locomotives but turned to the German firm of Krupp in West Germany for new locos and introduced diesel-hydraulic locomotives and new coaching stock from East Germany at a later stage.

The triangular Krupp builder's plate is prominent on the smokebox door of metre gauge 2-8-2 D52072 standing at Solo Balapan station with the afternoon mixed to Madiun on 4th August 1983. By this date the two daily return mixed trains between Solo and Madiun were the last regular steam hauled main line workings on the P.J.K.A. The loco seen here, D52072 was built in 1951, works number 3296. Photo: Keith R. Chester.

Locomotives of the Ambarawa Railway Museum

All photographs by Jim Grant.

Right: B2711, one of 16 0-4-2T delivered between 1912 and 1921 by Hartmann, formerly S.J.S. no. 201 and factory no. 3757 of 1914. The '2' beneath the loco number is the number in the Museum's roster.

The museum also has another S.J.S. locomotive, Klein-Lindner 0-8-0T, D1007, formerly S.J.S. 301, supplied by Hartmann in 1915 in a series of eleven locos delivered 1913-15 (not illustrated).

Below left: B2220, incorrectly numbered C2220, is an 0-4-2T for tramway service, formerly N.I.S. no. 306 and Hartmann 2568/1900. Twenty of these engines were built 1898-1900 half of which were still in service in the 1970s.

Above right: Hartmann delivered seven of these tramway 0-6-0T to the N.I.S. during the period 1899-1908. C1603 dates from 1902 and previously carried N.I.S. number 250.

Another 0-6-0T not illustrated, C1704, is also preserved at Ambarawa. Five examples of the type were built 1899-1902 by Hartmann.

Right: The sole member of its class, but appearing to differ very little from the class C16, 0-6-0T no. C1801 was formerly N.I.S. no. 259 and was also a Hartmann product (7151/1914).

Above left: In 1905 Beyer Peacock supplied 0-4-0 tram loco no. B2014, formerly S.C.S. no. 29. This was one of 19 such engines whose construction was shared between the Beyer Peacock and Werkspoor of Holland during the years 1900-07.

Above right: 0-6-2T C2001 represents one of the larger types of loco used by the N.I.S. on its 3'6" gauge tramway lines. Formerly N.I.S. 351, this example was one of ten built by Hartmann from 1902 to 1911, works no. 1795 of 1902.

2-6-0T in the museum include C1140 and C1240, representing the S.S. class 300 compound and class 400 simple locos illustrated elsewhere by the author.

Above: 2-6-2T no. C2407, formerly N.I.S. 271, was a Werkspoor product, one of fifteen such locomotives delivered 1908-11, nine of which still remained in service in 1973.

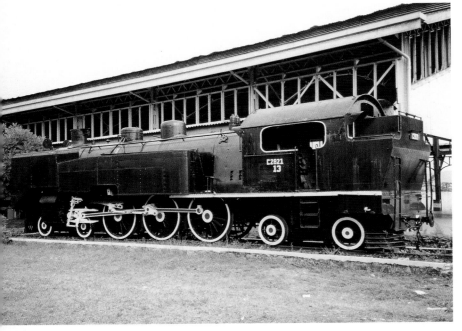

Left: The Staats Spoorwegen class 1300 4-6-4Ts were built by Henschel, Hartmann and Esslingen in 1921. Out of the total of 58 delivered, 57 remained in service as at the beginning of 1973, including C2841, Henschel 18175 of 1921.

The museum also has another 4-6-4T, C2728, which was originally S.S. 1110, built in 1919 by Werkspoor. Thirty-nine examples were supplied by SLM, Werkspoor and Armstrong-Whitworth 1916-22.

Right: Amongst the locomotives supplied by Beyer Peacock to the Netherlands Indies Railways (N.I.S.) were ten 4-6-0s delivered in 1912 and 1913, all of which continued to run into the 1970s. Class leader C5101 was originally N.I.S. 371.

Left: Beyer Peacock also built this 4-6-0, C5417, formerly S.C.S. no. 201, one of nineteen supplied to the Semarang Cheribon Stoomtram Mij by Beyer Peacock and Hartmann in 1922.

Former S.C.S. 0-4-0 no. 101 is also in the museum, the first of twenty-seven tender engines supplied by Hartmann 1908-13. It now carries P.J.K.A. no. B5210 and was Hartmann 3484 of 1911.

Right: Ten S.S. class 1500 2-8-2s were built by Hartmann and delivered in 1920, D5106 actually having been constructed in 1919, works no. 4138.

Not illustrated but also present at the museum is an S.S. class 600 2-cylinder compound 4-4-0, P.J.K.A. B5112, one of 44 delivered 1900-09 by Hanomag, Hartmann and Werkspoor.

Right: A machine local to Ambarawa, B25 class 0-4-2 rack and adhesion tank engine no. B2501, Esslingen 3242/1902. Five of these locos were supplied 1902-1905, some of which have latterly been in use for tourist and enthusiast specials, subject to local conditions of track maintenance and other matters. This rack tank and its coach are not actually in the museum itself but preserved at the Monumen Palagan Ambarawa.

Left: F1002 'Javanic' type 2-12-2T, formerly S.S. class 800 dating from 1915. Hanomag delivered 28 of these most successful mountain railway locomotives between 1912 and 1920 and members of the class were still active in the 1970s.

Right: S.S. class 1600 2-6-6-0 Mallet no. CC5029 was built by SLM at Winterthur, Switzerland in 1928, works no. 3249. Out of the 30 delivered by SLM and Werkspoor 1927-28, 25 remained in service in 1973. One of the Werkspoor examples has been returned to Holland and put on display at the railway museum in Utrecht.

Another Mallet is preserved at the Ambarawa museum, 0-4-4-2T BB1012, originally an S.S. class 500 built by Hartmann in 1907.

Notable Javan Steam Locomotives - the S.S. 900 and 1400 Classes

The State Railways (SS) of the then Dutch East Indies possessed a batch of medium sized 2-cylinder 'Consolidation' type of freight tender locomotives of the series 900 introduced by the System from 1914 until 1921, having been developed by the then Technical Bureau of the Department of the Colonies in collaboration with the German locomotive firm of Hanomag. The firm, long since defunct, ceased steam locomotive construction in 1928 to concentrate on the manufacture of heavy road transport motor vehicles and was one of the builders participating in the construction of 42 locomotives. The other firms were Werkspoor of Amsterdam, the Swiss Locomotive and Machine Works, and Hartmann of Germany. The locomotives possessed wide fire-boxes to burn indigenous coal of low caloric value necessitating a high boiler centre over rail, the second highest on the system. As the service speed was a moderate 50 km/h (30 mph), balancing of the motion was kept to a minimum with all drivers evenly balanced. Notable features were the uneven driver spacing and plenty of 'daylight' under the boiler, features which in the opinion of the writer were pleasing to look at and these locomotives were therefore a favourite of mine. They could be found all over the system pulling freight trains on the plains.

They had a strong exhaust blast and these engines departing at the head of a long goods train under a cannonade of exhaust beats was a joy to behold. Presumably on account of the strong exhaust these locomotives belonged to the few which still carried a wire-netting spark arrester on their chimney. The engines always looked immaculate with bright boilerbands and polished 'Russian Iron' boiler jackets which gave them a bluish shine. They still carried cillaterns, even at that time when I knew them, until they were given express train duties, after having undergone extensive modifications of the running gear and draughting to make them suitable for such duties. They emerged from the shops with stovepipe chimney and oversized elephant-eared smoke deflection fitted, which features in the opinion of the author did not improve their looks. They were then given electric lighting.

During the 'Depression' of the late Twenties and the greater part of the Thirties a goodly number of these engines in their original state went into storage, only to gradually come out of store when the economic climate showed signs of improving towards the close of the Thirties decade. Also during that period the railways had to cope with ever increasing road competition and in order to meet this challenge the railways had to improve on train

Right: The 1400 class 2-8-2T. Staats Spoorwegen locomotive no. 1414 built by Werkspoor (500/1922) later renumbered to D1414.

Below: The 900 class 2-8-0. S.S. no. 932 was Werkspoor no. 481 of 1921 and latterly P.N.K.A. loco D5028.

Works photographs courtesy of Ian G.T. Duncan.

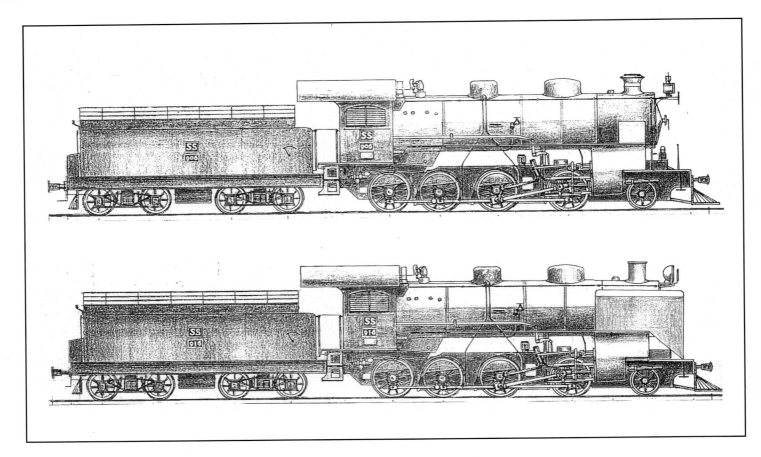

The series 900 2-8-0 in its original state and as reconstructed. Drg: J.R.

services and timings, speeding up trains towards the close of the decade, like everywhere else in the world . The Administration therefore introduced improved services between the major centres by raising train speeds to 90 km/hr and by laying on short fast trains such as 'The Speedy Four' and 'The Speedy Five' trains i.e. 4 or 5 fast services in both directions between the larger centres. To implement these new services the railway administration was looking around for a suitable locomotive. Obtaining new locomotives was out of the question and the choice therefore fell on the

900 and 1400 classes, the 1400 class being the tank version of the 900 class. The two classes were to all intents and purposes of identical construction. As the above mentioned locomotives were whiling away their existence in storage, 30 of them were duly hauled into the workshops to be modified and improved upon for the intended services.

As these two classes had only small diameter wheels of 1,105 mm (3'6"), the 1400 class being a heavy shunting locomotive, re-balancing the running gear for sustained 90 km/hr running posed a problem but was satisfactorily solved by cutting out the old balancing weights and welding in new weights. This careful balancing kept 'hammerblow' at that speed within bounds. Also these locomotives had leading 'Adams' axles which gave no trouble at all at speed and the engines after re-balancing rode like coaches, even on 105 km/hr test runs. Draughting was improved by 'opening out' and internal streamlining and fire-boxes were improved for better combustion. Furthermore these locomotives were ballasted with an extra 2 tons of weight in order to increase trac-tion and acceleration when starting. All these modifications incorporated into a basically 'goods engine' made them a success story. Bystanders observing these locomotives at speed spoke of 'a mist of flaying rods'.

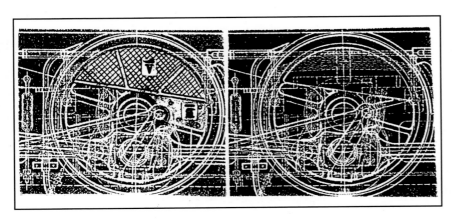

Re-balancing the main driver on the 900 class.
On the left is the original counterweight, with the new one on the right.
A: Counterweight cut out, pockets filled with lead, and sideplates welded on.
B: Additional counterweight built up and riveted then welded in.

In certain respects the pre-war State Railways of the then Dutch East-Indies were a trend setter in locomotive matters and train running in South East Asia. The originator of all locomotive improvements on the State railways during that period was Engineer Berg who tragically ended his life before a Japanese firing squad being accused by the occupying forces of sabotage. In hindsight some railway men wondered for how long these lokies could withstand the thrashing before wear and tear would take its toll, but in the humble opinion of the writer the foregoing was a prelude to dieselisation (DMU's) had the War not intervened. The 900 class had a long and useful career spanning two World Wars until withdrawn and scrapped in the Seventies. In the post-war period the remaining engines reverted back to more mundane duties. The author takes it that at least one example is preserved in the Ambarawa Railway Museum of the Indonesian State Railways on the Island of Java.

S.S. 2-8-0 no. 902 shows its modified counterweights but still has the original chimney and has not yet received smoke deflectors. The maker's plate is clearly visible, Hanomag, Hannover-Linden number 7154, dated 1914.
Photo: author's collection.

Fully modified 2-8-0 no. 931. In addition to the heavier counterweights an extra two tons of ballast had been added to the series 900 in order to improve traction and acceleration when starting.
Photo: author's collection.

The Mallet Locomotive in Java

It could be said that the Island of Java was Mallet country, the State Railways at one time or another possessing this type of steam locomotive with many different wheel-arrangements. The Mallet (compound) locomotive, compound between brackets as all Mallets are compound locomotives, was the brainchild of the Frenchman Anatole Mallet who never financially benefited from his invention. The locomotive either in tank or tender version invariably consisted of a fixed frame carrying the high pressure cylinders and the rear part of the boiler, and a frame carrying the front part of the boiler via a sliding support and also carrying the low pressure cylinders. The forward frame was connected to the fixed frame via a hinge pin, enabling it to swing out left and right to follow the curvature of the track This type was therefore ideally suited for mountainous terrain with sharp curvature and steep gradients requiring high tractive effort. (See diagram). Invariably the Mallet was a 4-cylinder compound locomotive. The interconnection of the high and low pressure cylinders was via flexible steam piping as the steam was first supplied to the high-pressure cylinders on the fixed frame and then passed to the forward cylinders on the articulated frame.

During the first decades of the 20th century the Mallet became popular in North America where they constructed approximately 2,000 of this type of locomotive and where they grew to unprecedented size. As time progressed compounding was discarded and high pressure cylinders were substituted for the LP cylinders so they became simply "Articulated" and grew even bigger in size. The largest steam locomotive in the world was an articulated and it is a sobering thought that the last steam locomotive in revenue service in the USA was one of these. The first Mallets on Java were of the tank type, therefore carrying their own fuel and water supply on the locomotive itself. The later more modern and larger Mallet locomotives were of the tender type.

The first Mallets of the 0-4-4-2 wheel arrangement were introduced in 1901, followed by 2-6-6-0s in 1908, all constructed by European manufacturers. There were two versions of this latter type, the second version was constructed by Werkspoor as their first attempt at constructing Mallet locomotives.

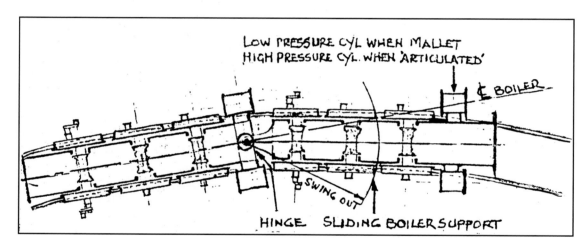

The form of articulation used for Mallet compound and simple expansion locomotives.

A prime example of the Mallet locomotive, Staats Spoorwegen no. 1207 built by the American Locomotive Company (56160/1916). This large metre gauge loco was later renumbered to DD5007. Works photograph courtesy of Ian G.T. Duncan.

*One of the early series of Mallets, 0-4-4-0T BB1012 was built by Hartmann in 1906 but still active at
Ambarawa on 24th January 1972. Photo: D. Trevor Rowe.*

The 'American Locomotive Company' (Alco) Mallet

The Mallet locomotive came really into its stride with the
introduction of the large American Locomotive Company's 2-
8-8-0 in 1916 of the series 1201-1208, followed by the second
series 1209-1220 in 1920, also from Alco. Then the
Administration turned away from the American builder in favour
of European manufacturers. These European locomotives
comprised the series 1251-1260 2-8-8-0s of 1923, followed by the
2-6-6-0 series 1600 of 1928 comprising 30 locomotives, also
from European builders, both series to be described in the following section. The series 1600 Mallets were the last Mallets to be
ordered for the Javan system.

The writer observed many a member of these Mallet classes at
Solo Djèbrès except for the series 1251-1260 which locomotives
went into storage before writer's time. It was so, that all the large
2-8-8-0 Mallets of both American and European origin went into
storage at the onset of or during the Great Depression at the close
of the twentieth decade due to diminishing traffic only to come
gradually out of storage again as the Depression abated towards
the close of the thirties decade. The series 1251-1260 of European
origin only came out of storage in 1938, and shortly after the
family moved back to Europe never to return.

It is on record that the original Alco series 1201-1208 never
turned a wheel again after going into storage and were gradually
dismantled presumably to supply spare parts for the later Alcos.
All was not well with the Alco 2-8-8-0's. As speed and load
increased so did water and fuel consumption at vulgar rate. They
suffered from unequal power output of HP & LP cylinders and

from that bane of the Mallet locomotive called 'backpressure'
and, as a consequence, from frame cracking of the front low pressure unit brought about by 'pounding'. Pounding can be attributed
to many causes but the prime cause might have been the high
backpressure. Being of American construction the frames were of
the bar frame type following American practice of the time. As a
matter of note, these American built Mallets introduced electric
lighting to State Railway system locomotives

In the second decade after the turn of the Century, when the
Javan 2-8-8-0 Mallets were built, the Mallet locomotive gained
popularity in the USA, being an answer to high tractive effort at
low speed. They grew to immense proportions, like the Virginian
Ry 2-10-10-2 with a size of boiler never surpassed and the largest
cylinders ever fitted on a steam locomotive. As things stood in
Java, there was a lot of tinkering with LP cylinder bores i.e.
HP/LP cylinder ratios, but to no avail. The brutes remained
cantankerous, until the State Railway's Test Department for
Rolling Stock got hold of them and started an intensive test
programme in order to improve the performance of these locomotives, then the largest on the system.

The Test Department stood under the guidance of Engineer de
Gruijter who could be likened to the O.S. Ell of the system but
then two and a half decades earlier. O.S. Ell was the post-war
British locomotive front-end expert of Great Western Railway
fame. Engineer de Gruijter was an aerodynamics expert in his
own right and that is what it is all about with streamlining of locomotive front-end steam circuits. The Department succeeded in
raising the power output by 20% in the process, altering valve

events and making changes to the starting valve as well as other changes including modifying the blastpipe arrangement. They emerged from the shops carrying a Duplex exhaust which improved their looks as well as their steaming ability. Their power output hovered round about 1,700 HP. Like any self-respecting Mallet of that period the HP cylinders had piston valves driven by Walschaerts gear and the LP cylinders had 'Richardson' balanced slide-valves also driven by Walschaerts gear. The steam powered reverse gear was of the 'Mellin' type, these locomotive being the only ones on the system to be fitted with power-reverse gears. Mellin at the time was a consulting engineer for the American Locomotive Company.

The amount of steam exhausted was so enormous that each cylinder required its own flexible exhaust piping, the two pipes converting into a single blastpipe. Some of the locomotives of the second series like no. 1217 and no. 1218 were provided with 'Duplex' mechanical stokers. They were transformed into the most impressive steam locomotives on the system and most favourite of the author, who still considers the 'Mallet' the king of all steam locomotives. The first series of Alco Mallets nos. 1201-1208 never received the 'treatment'. Was simpling ever considered like in the USA? Probably, but why should a costly casting like the LP-cylinder block be discarded when only requiring re-boring or re-sleeving? These locomotives were reconstructed in

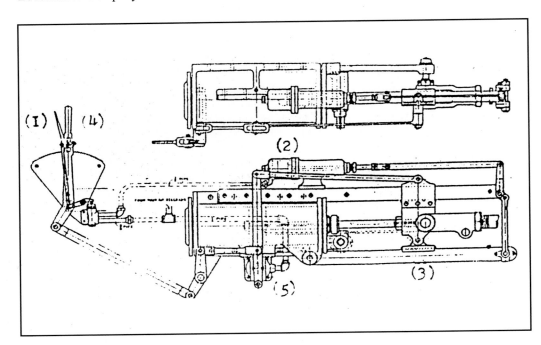

Operation of the Mellin steam reverser:
Squeeze latch on handle (1).
Steam is admitted to the spring loaded clamping bar cylinder (2).
The clamping bar releases the crosshead (3).
Move the reverser handle forward or reverse (4).
Valve (5) admits steam into the reverser cylinder.
The reverser piston moves forward or reverse, acting on the valve gear.
Release latch and the spring loading of (2) locks the reverser in position with the locking bar (3).

the late Twenties (1927) and the dark clouds of the 'Great Depression' were already gathering so these locomotives would shortly become excess baggage and remain so during the greater part of a decade.

These Mallets were large for the 3'6" (1,067 mm) gauge at the time, appearing immense to an impressionable young lad, but of course of 'Bantam' size compared with the US giants. 'Dusty Durrant in one of his articles stated that they were scaled down versions of the B&O Ry 2-8-8-0 Mallets and the writer would like to add that they must have had features borrowed from an earlier 2-8-8-2 Mallet built by the American Locomotive Company for the Brazilian 'Paulista' Railway in 1913. The author took the 'Paulista' photograph, inclined the LP cylinders, did away with the rear running wheels and a great likeness appeared.

The Javan Alco Mallets spent their entire careers on the torturous west Javan Preanger Mountain Line with its 3% grades and 200 metre radius curves (compensated), between Purwakarta and Padalarang. They pulled the expresses running between Batavia and Bandung until displaced by the European built series 1251-1260 Mallets and were relegated to goods services from then on.

As mentioned earlier some of the engines were provided with 'Duplex' mechanical stokers but when these wore out, being not entirely successful in service, they were not replaced and the engines rode with a compliment of two firemen and sometimes

three, thriving on a diet of coal briquettes. Wasteful? Those days labour was cheap and at least some employment was provided during the greater part of a difficult socio-economic period. Notwithstanding the initial steaming troubles, frame cracking and other maladies so peculiar to the Mallet, they gave sterling service and lasted well into the late sixties when they were taken out of service, their melodious chime whistle once echoing through the west Javan mountains stilled forever. Regretfully not one of these Alco Mallets has been preserved.

Was the 'Garratt' locomotive ever considered? Perhaps only as a possible replacement, because when these 2-8-8-0s were introduced in 1916 the Mallet locomotive was already well established with the Garratt locomotive still being in its infancy. With hindsight the Garratt would have been an ideal traction vehicle on the Preanger Mountain lines, with their multitude of spindly trestles and viaducts allowing only light axle loads and the Garratt configuration allowing a more generous spread of axle loading and having better curving ability. Due to its light axle loading (12-13 tons) the Mallets required 16 driving wheels compacted under one boiler. Probably a 2-6-2+2-6-2 Garratt would have sufficed, but this is conjecture. De Gruijter's opinion was that probably the Mallet was thermodynamically the more economic machine and he should know.

A European and an American built Mallet locomotive in Java in 1971. Leading is 2-6-6-0T CC1007 built by Hartmann in 1905, hauling out for photography 2-8-8-0 DD5110, constructed by Alco in 1919 but out of service by the time this picture was taken. Photo: A.E. Durrant.

The European-built Mallets

In the preceding section we saw that the State Railways administration ceased ordering Mallet locomotives from North American locomotive manufacturers and turned in 1923 to European based suppliers for further 2-8-8-0 Mallet locomotives.

The European Mallets comprised the 1251-1260 series, numbering 10 locomotives. Before the introduction of the re-routed 'Een-Daagse' Express (Daylight Express), in 1929, running throughout the length of the Island of Java between the administrative capitol of Batavia and the commercial capitol of Surabaya, (via

Staats Spoorwegen 2-8-8-0 compound Mallet no. 1255 built by the Saxon Locomotive Works, formerly Richard Hartmann.

2-8-8-0 DD5207, built at the Hartmann works in 1924, modified later, and in fine fettle at Tasikmalaja towards the western end of Java on 23rd January 1972. Photo: D. Trevor Rowe.

Cheribon, Purwokerto, and Kroja - see map), there existed an earlier Express running between Bandung and Surabaya via Tjitjalenka, Banjar and Kroja introduced in 1908 and called the 'Java Express'. This earlier express had to negotiate 150 km of torturous mountain country between Bandung and Banjar with gradients of 25‰ and 200 metre radius curves. These ten locomotives were principally ordered for this line to speed up the express timings as the Alco Mallets were found to be too slow footed.

Main Dimensions:

HP cylinder diameter	450 mm
LP cylinder diameter	700 mm
Piston stroke	610 mm
Driving wheel diameter	1,102 mm
Boiler pressure	14 atm
Grate area	4.1 m²
Loco weight empty	85.5 tons
Loco weight in service	95.5 tons
Adhesion weight	87.5 tons

Three manufacturers participated in their construction namely the firms of Hanomag in Germany, the Saxon Locomotive Works

(formerly Richard Hartmann), also in Germany, and Werkspoor of Amsterdam, the lion's share of the order going to Werkspoor. The design was prepared by Hanomag. 'Hanomag' stands for Hannoversche Maschinenbau AG. (Hannover Machine Works Ltd) established in the German town of Hannover. In 1928 this well known firm closed its locomotive manufacturing department which was then taken over by the equally well known German locomotive builders of Henschel & Sohn, established in the town of Magdeburg. Hanomag after the re-organisation concentrated on the manufacture of heavy road vehicles and became famous for their gun tractors or half-tracks of World War Two. Before winding up locomotive building Hanomag supplied many a steam locomotive to the Javan State Railways (SS). The European built 2-8-8-0 Mallets were virtually identical in size and make up to the Alco Mallets except for having plate frames instead of bar frames and having piston valves fitted on the LP cylinders instead of the more usual LP slide valves fitted on Mallets of that period. As can be seen from photographs, some members of the class of European Mallets were provided with round sand domes, others were fitted with square sand boxes. In looks the round sand domes suited the engines better than the square sand boxes.

These European Mallets suffered even more than the Alco Mallets from unequal power output from the HP and LP cylinders.

A most undesirable trait of the Mallet locomotive came to the fore in that by increasing speed and load, the rear HP unit would get into a spin and thus raise the receiver cylinder pressure, which caused the front LP unit to slip, which in its turn lowered the receiver pressure again, causing the rear HP unit to get in another frenzy, and so on ad infinitum. This phenomenon is beautifully recorded on O. Winston Link's LP record 'The 2nd Pigeon and the Mocking Bird' of the Norfolk & Western Y-class Mallet on a mine run.

This circumstance in the case of the SS Mallet was mainly brought about by the starting valve being coupled to the reach rod, admitting high pressure boiler steam into the receiver at 65% HP cylinder steam admission. The USA Norfolk & Western Ry had this worked out to a fine art on their latest Y-class Mallets towards the close of the steam era on this railway in the late fifties. For this reason Engineer De Gruijter of the SS Test Department chose a member of the type 2-8-8-0 Mallet class as his guinea-pig in his attempts to improve the North American and European Mallet classes. How admirably he succeeded in doing so, by skilfully tinkering with valve events, increasing steam admission to the HP and LP cylinders, raising superheating temperature, separating the starting valve from the reach rod and working it manually, doubling the exhaust and other changes. The locomotive was now able to gyrate the expresses of ever increasing weight round the tight curves in the mountains at increased speed. The reconstruction of this first European Mallet was so successful that all Mallets of American and European construction followed suit except for the first series Alcos 1201-1208. The author ever regrets never having seen the European Mallet as these locomotives went into limbo early during the Great Depression to come out again late 1938.

Most of the locomotive testing during the reconstruction on the Mallets was done on the Purwakarta - Padalarang line with a continuous grade of 16‰ (1.6%) or 1:62 over a distance of 45 km. The State Railways were large enough and prosperous enough to afford a test coach or dynamometer car, as a matter of fact testing was an on-going affair including all major classes during the mid-twenties and the following thirties. That was the time that most, if not all, principal locomotive classes appeared

with modified chimneys, with smoke deflectors, and when the State Railways fully worked out plans to dieselise after 1941. That was also the time that some well liked classes disappeared from Solo Junction to take up duties elsewhere in the country after reconstruction.

It would be appropriate to explain that the Continentals express their gradients in pro-mille (‰) and the Americans in percentage (%) or in feet per hundred. The following is a table expressing ruling gradients on the Preanger main lines:

Purwakarta-Padalarang 16‰
Bandung - Tjibatu - Tasikmalaya - Banjar - Maos 25‰
Buitenzorg (Bogor) - Tjitjurug - Sukabumi 25‰
Sukabumi - Tjiantjur - Bandung 40‰

16 ‰ = 1.6% = 1:62
25‰ = 2.5% = 1:40
40‰ = 4.0% = 1:25

As a trial nos. 1251 & 1260 were fitted with a Worthington feedwater heater, but it was found that there was no marked added economy of the so fitted locomotives over the rest of the class, so these devices were removed. Neither did they receive mechanical stokers and they stayed hand fired all their life. They were provided with screw-reversers with a generously sized hand-wheel. Attempts were made at oil firing these locomotives but this came to naught as the copper fireboxes required too extensive refractory brickwork and the oil-fire being deleterious to the copper plating. From then on they were mainly fired with coal-briquettes and they thrived on it. Originally they were provided with 'Lambert' sanding gear (sand and water) but this device was found wanting and a compressed air sander of the German 'Knorr' type was provided. This device worked satisfactorily in the damp mountains and the rest of the class was so fitted. The last of these locomotives were taken out of service in the early seventies, long enough to give Messrs A.E. Durrant and Nick Lera time to record their exploits on film and video. The writer is not aware of one of these Mallets having been preserved.

S.S. 2-8-8-0 Mallet locomotive no. 1260 with a Worthington BL feedwater heater. Drg: J.R.

The 1600 Series Mallet

Having described the large 2-8-8-0 Mallet locomotives in the preceding sections, we come now to the Mallets of the 2-6-6-0 wheel arrangement which were ordered for the Javan State Railways (SS) in 1928. The State Railways at the time was desirous of having a medium weight Mallet locomotive with an 11 ton axle load for service on those mountain lines which did not allow the 12 ton axle load of the 2-8-8-0 Mallets and to relieve the ageing Mallet tank locomotives of the 0-4-4-2 and 2-6-6-0 wheel arrangements whose pulling power fell short of what was desired.

They were the last Mallets to be ordered for this railway and the most modern of the trio of classes. These Mallets were developed by the Bureau of Engineering of the then State Department of the Colonies acting as 'Crown Agent' for the SS, in conjunction with the Schweizerische Lokomotiv und Maschinenfabrik, abbreviated SLM (Swiss Locomotive and Machine Works). SLM of Winterthur, Switzerland designed the locomotives and built the lion's share of the 30 examples ordered, with Werkspoor participating in the construction of 10 locomotives.

Besides the usual vacuum, steam, and hand brakes, these locomotives were also provided with the 'Riggenbach' compression brake (working only) on the high pressure cylinders, the low pressure cylinders sucking in atmosphere air via a bypass valve fitted on the blastpipe and pumping this air into the receiver pipe connected to the exhaust cavities of the HP cylinders. By laying the reverser in full reverse, the HP cylinders started to compress this air, the work done in doing so braking off the engine whilst descending long gradients. A regulating throttle valve was provided in the exhaust line, which line was connected to the broad lipped chimney, this lip being provided with outlet holes acting as a silencer. In order to cool the HP cylinders when generating heat in compressing the air, water was injected into these cylinders. Also a 'Knorr' type steam compressor was provided to supply compressed air for the sanding gear, as was successfully fitted on the European series of 2-8-8-0 Mallet locomotives previously described.

All 30 locomotives were provided with feedwater heaters, 15 locomotives so fitted with the French ACFI type (L'Industrie) and 15 locomotives with the 'Worthington' type. Apparently these devices must have been working satisfactorily as the author observed the engines so fitted frequenting Solo Djèbrès station and yard right up to 1939. A goodly number of these engines lost their feed apparatus, which equipment was then placed on the rejuvenated Swiss built 'Pacifics' of the 700 series in order to enhance their performance on the improved express train timings in the late thirties.

The Mallets were thoroughly modern locomotives, at the time incorporating modern views on steam locomotive design, in particular as regards compounding, in view of the test results obtained from the 2-8-8-0 series of Mallets. However, why the Design Department of the Department of the Colonies opted to perpetuate the Mallet compound system instead of 'simpling' 4 sets of cylinders escaped the Writer. Except for the USA's Norfolk & Western Railway, who stuck to a good thing in their 'Y' class 2-8-8-2 Mallets, steadily improving these locomotives, Mallet compounding was 'as dead as a Dodo' in the USA. Probably the Administration was of the opinion that using steam twice over would be more economical that simple expansion in view of chronic locomotive fuel supply problems at the time.

Having served as mountain locomotives in the Western Javan Preanger Mountains and elsewhere, the 1600 series Mallets were assigned new jobs in the mid thirties pulling fast heavy goods trains on the Javan Plains, especially in the vicinity of the capitol of Batavia, speeding up train timings. Probably the Administration took a leaf out of the Union Pacific book, who used their 'Challenger' 4-6-6-4 articulateds on 'Fast Timings' at the time. Maximum speed of these bantam-sized SS Mallets was set at 60 km/hour (approx. 40 mph) but approaching that speed they started objecting to it by becoming 'lively runners', probably brought about by their lightness. 'Big Boy' articulation technology was still a decade away.

The writer can vouch for this 'Bronco' attitude as on one particular morning he and a friend cycled to a large four span railway bridge outside Solo spanning the Solo River, Java's longest and largest river. Ignoring the bridge's 'No Trespassing' sign the two lads proceeded on foot towards the centre of the bridge till their attention was caught by a 'Local' standing on the Eastern river bank, shouting and wildly gesticulating and pointing in an

S.S. 1600 series 2-6-6-0 Mallet tender locomotive with an ACFI feedwater heater. Photo courtesy of SLM, author's collection.

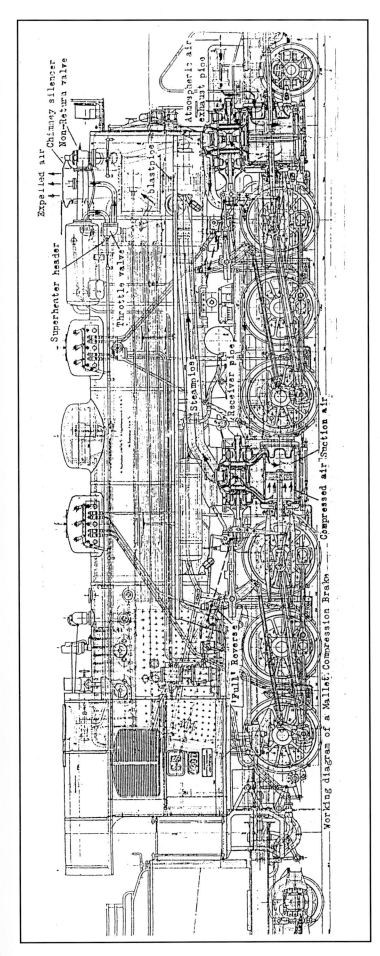

— Working diagram of a Mallet. Compression Brake —— Compressed air 'Suction air

Labels on diagram: Expelled air, Chimney silencer, Non-Return valve, Atmospheric air exhaust pipe, Superheater header, Blastpipe, Throttle valve, Steam log, Receiver pipe, Full Reverse

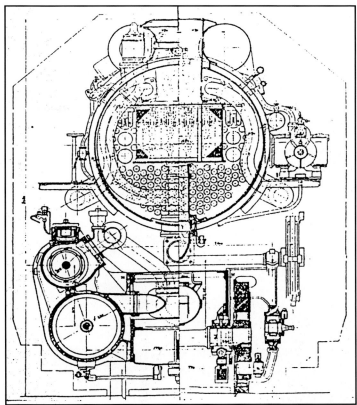

Above: Front view of the 1600 class Mallet with ACFI feedwater heater fitted beside boiler.

Functioning of a 1600 class Mallet compression brake (see diagram above).

The locomotive is moving forward with the regulator closed.
The swivel-jointed LP exhaust pipe to the blastpipe is opened to the atmosphere and blastpipe closed.
The LP piston moves backward sucking in atmospheric air into the front of the LP cylinder via the exhaust port and front steam port.
Air trapped behind the LP piston is pumped to the front of the HP cylinder via the LP rear steam port and the LP cylinder steam inlet into the receiver pipe (which is connected from the HP cylinder exhaust ports and LP cylinder steam inlet).
Air trapped behind the HP piston is compressed via the HP rear steam port and steam inlet into the steampipe and superheater header and hence via a connecting pipe and throttling valve into the chimney silencer.
All cylinders have been provided with pressure relief valves.

easterly direction. Looking up, there it was, a black monster bearing on the lads at speed. Now the race to get off the bridge pronto was on, and just in time, as in a flash a 1600 series Mallet and its train thundered off the bridge Solo-bound with its front-unit heaving and hunting under the swaying locomotive, the chime-whistle yelling. A brown fist was shaken at the two lads from out of the cab-window. Phew!! Understandably, as from that time on No Trespassing signs were viewed with more respect.

After World War 2 the engines returned to their old stamping ground shorn of feedwater apparatus and possibly other gadgets and they lasted well into the late seventies, long enough to have

their exploits recorded on ciné, still film and video by Messrs. Nick Lera, 'Dusty' Durrant and others. Happy to say that at least one specimen built by Werkspoor was preserved for posterity and returned to her country of birth, donated by the present Indonesian State Railways. It is on display standing in the Railway Museum of the Netherlands in Utrecht after having undergone a 'cosmetic' refit carried out by the Meiningen steamshop in Germany, however, the engine is not in running condition. She bears the nameplate 'Sri Gunug', the Javanese name for 'Queen of the Mountains'.

Close up view of a 1600 series Mallet fitted with a Worthington feedwater heater. Photo: author's collection.

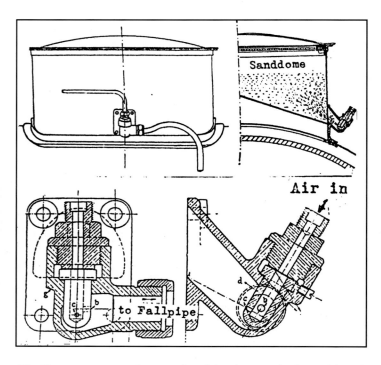

The Knorr compressed air sander, the only one which would work satisfactorily in the damp western Javan Preanger Mountains. The secret lies in nozzle C which loosens the sand in the sand dome and nozzle B which blows the sand into the fallpipe and onto the rails. The extra steam compressor to be carried on an otherwise vacuum braked engine was still worthwhile.

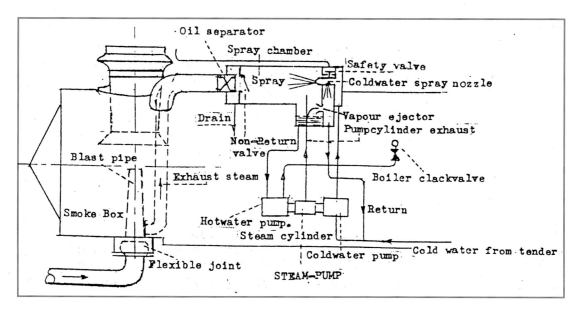

Left: Working diagram of a Worthington feedwater installation. Drg: J.R.

The Rack Line to the Coalfields

Mention has been made earlier of the difficulties encountered by the Staats Spoorwegen in providing suitable fuel. In the formative years wood fuel was used but gradually the S.S. introduced steam coal imported from South Africa, Australia, Bengal, or Japan. In 1921 coal imports ceased and the S.S. went over to coal supplied from indigenous sources, mainly from West Sumatran coalfields like 'Ombilin', whose coal burned satisfactorily in locomotive fireboxes.

In September 1887 the then Dutch Parliament had passed an Act authorising the construction of a railway line at government expense from Brandewijna Baai (Brandy Bay), on Sumatra's west coast to the extensive interior coalfields, the so-called 'Ombilin'

coalfields near Sawah Lunto in the Padang Highlands. The line covered a distance of 155 km and was complete with coal loading facilities at Emma Haven (Emma Harbour) on Brandewijna Baai. There are other coalfields on Sumatra but the writer would like to expound on this railway only, as the Javan Railways mainly consumed Ombilin coal. The line was laid in the 3'6" (1067 mm) gauge and crossed two mountain ranges provided with rack sections of a total length of 35 km. The total length of this railway including branch lines came to 284 km. Emma Haven had a coal staithe which also provided bunkering facilities for sea-going vessels. A large locomotive depot was established at Padang Pandjang, stabling 38 rack locomotives at one time or another.

Kolenpakhuis Emmahaven.

The coal facility at Emmahaven. The loco pushing the wagons is thought to be one of the Sumatra Staats Spoorwegen 2-6-0Ts built by Esslingen 1892-1904, later on the DKA type C33.
Postcard view courtesy of Christopher Walker.

Kabelbaan O. M. te Sawah Loento

The cableway to Sawah Lunto, near the top of the Sumatran coal system.
Postcard view courtesy of Christopher Walker.

SUMATRA
1925

SUMATRA EAST-COAST.
MALACCA-
STRAITS

INDIAN OCEAN

SUMATRA WEST-COAST

The rack section was of with the Riggenbach ladder type invented by Nicholas Riggenbach (1817-1899), a Swiss railway engineer and the World's foremost rack railway expert. The construction engineer of the line was the capable Dutch railway engineer A. Kuntze. The line he built reaches its maximum gradient of 8% or 1 in 12 at a height of 1,154 metres above sea level, between the volcanoes Merapi and Singgalan. The main line to the coast over which coal transport took place had a maximum gradient of 7%, or 1 in 14. In the year 1917 the so far autonomous Sumatra Staats Spoorwegen came under the direct management of the Java Staats Spoorwegen, with the mines under the Department of Mines.

In the formative years small indirect driven rack locomotives were used, i.e. the two (outside) cylinders drove a pair of adhesion wheels with the coupling rods split to drive the cog wheel engaging on the rack rail and the next pair of adhesion wheels. This gave peculiar problems as now the diameters of the adhesion wheels had to match that of the cog wheel, the adhesion wheel diameters possibly differing in small amounts when there was a newly re-profiled wheel and a worn wheel. Any difference in circumferential speed between the cog and adhesion wheels had to be made up by slippage of the adhesion wheels, with the attendant increase in wheel maintenance. The speed capabilities were low, at 10 km/h. This speed also had to be maintained on rackless sections as higher speeds could cause the cog wheel equipment to be damaged.

Left: The rack railway entering a tunnel in the difficult Anei Gorge section with its steep inclines, sharp curvature, and high bridges..
Photo: author's collection.

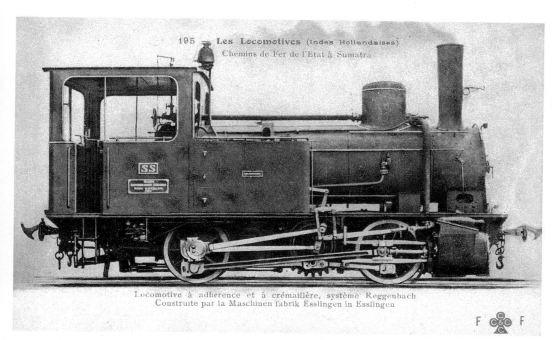

195 — Les Locomotives (Indes Hollandaises)
Chemins de Fer de l'Etat à Sumatra

SS

Locomotive à adhérence et à crémaillère, système Reggenbach
Construite par la Maschinen fabrik Esslingen in Esslingen

F ☘ F

A two cylinder, indirect drive, rack and adhesion 0-4-0T of the Sumatran State Railways. Esslingen built seven such locos 1893-1905, SSS numbers 61, 62, 66-68, 70 & 71. They ran until 1921 when larger engines became available. Postcard view courtesy of Christopher Walker.

Right: working diagram of an indirect drive rack loco:
A=rack gear drive shaft.
D=connecting rod.
K1=coupling rod to rack gear.
K2=coupling rod to leading adhesion axle.
Drg: J.R.

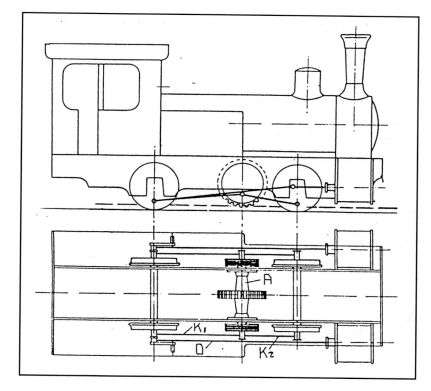

In 1913 some larger rack and adhesion locomotives of the 0-8-2 wheel notation and with divided drive were introduced, built by Esslingen in Germany and SLM in Switzerland. They were four-cylinder compound locomotives, i.e. with a pair of cylinders driving the adhesion wheels exhausting into a pair of cylinders driving the rack wheels. A pinion wheel was driven by the low pressure cylinders and this then drove onto the cog wheel, but as the tooth ration was 1:2 the rack drive ran at twice the speed of the adhesion drive, so the compound cylinders could be of the same bore as the high pressure adhesion cylinders. Running on adhesion track only, the rack machinery was shut down and the engine ran as simple expansion.

The 0-8-2 locos were followed by 0-10-0 'ten-couplers', also four-cylinder compounds. The 0-10-0 rack tanks were truly magnificent pieces of steam engineering, capable of dragging 130 gross tons up the incline. Speed on the rack section increased from 10 km/h (indirect drive locos) to 15 km/h (independent drive locos). On adhesion only stretches the maximum speed was set at 40 km/h. The 0-10-0 rack and adhesion locomotives were provided with Riggenbach counter-pressure brakes working on all four cylinders and the engine was able to restrain a 180 ton train on a 7% gradient. After the introduction of these 0-10-0 rack locos the older and obsolete indirect drive locomotives

were retired (by 1930).

The writer, having encountered rack locomotives in Java and in post-war Europe, regrettably never had the opportunity at the time or afterwards to visit this highly interesting railway. It fell into decline due to high transport costs, passing through an intermediate period of oil-firing on the Javan railways and the de-steaming of the railway in the seventies and eighties. Even in the post-war period of the late forties of being employed on Sumatra's east coast made it impossible to visit due to impenetrable jungle and impassable mountain ranges. In the 1970s the last of these locos were caught on video by Nick Lera and in still pictures by 'Dusty' Durrant.

Sumatran Staats Spoorwegen no. 56, an indirect drive 0-4-2 rack and adhesion tank loco, built at Esslingen (3068/1902). Photo courtesy of Christopher Walker.

SS no. 117, an 0-10-0 4 cylinder compound rack and adhesion loco built by Esslingen. (Author's collection).

SLM built SS no. 103, a four cylinder compound 0-8-2 rack and adhesion tank loco. (Author's collection).

Northern Sumatra and The Deli Railway Company

The writer of this account proceeded to the Dutch East Indies shortly after the 2nd World War as a budding engineer to take up employment with a large company engaged in the rehabilitation of its numerous plantations on the tropical island of Sumatra, left in disarray after the ravages caused by the Japanese Military occupation. The author was stationed on a large sisal plantation near Pematang Siantar, the district capital of Simelungan, roughly 150 km south east of Medan, then the provincial capital of Deli in northern Sumatra. That particular fertile area of the northern Sumatra was and is still dotted with large plantations or estates, established during the close of the last century and the first decades of this century, literally hacked out of the virgin jungle and producing valuable palm oil, rubber, sisal fibre, tea and tobacco for export. The area around Medan in particular was famous for producing the world renowned Cigar Tobacco Leaf the so called 'Deli Dekblad' (outer wrapping of the Cigar). When I say large plantation, I mean large as this particular establishment and its adjacent sister plantation counted a working population of nearly 2,000 souls and possessed about 150 km of narrow gauge railway and over 28 steam locos ranging from small 0-4-0 tank engines to 0-4-4-0 Mallet compound tank locos and heavy 2-cylinder rigid framed 0-10-0s coupled to four wheeled tenders.

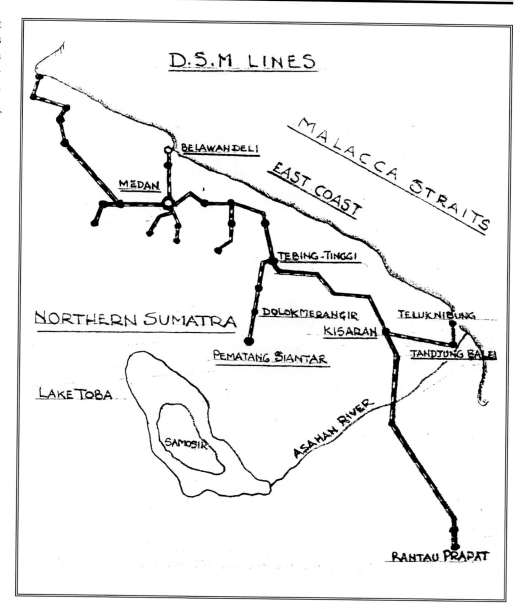

These last locomotives were provided with the patented Klien-Linder radially adjusting driving axles, making these engines very flexible in the usual tight curves of a narrow gauge railway.

Both estates had access to a siding on the Indonesian standard 1,067 mm (3'6") gauge Medan-Pematang Siantar main line of the then privately owned Deli Spoorweg Maatschappij, abbreviated DSM (Deli Railway Company), now a fallen flag railway having been absorbed into the Indonesian State Railways. The access line to the neighbouring sister estate and the aforementioned standard gauge railhead crossed a deep ravine on an impressively high viaduct. The Deli Railway Company possessed only 2-cylindered, wood fired tank locomotives of the 2-4-2, 2-6-4, and 2-8-4 wheel arrangements, and some oddities

Sisal Plantation.
Photo: J.R.

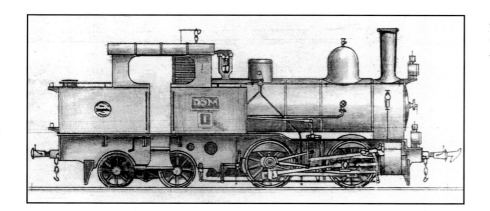

D.S.M. 0-4-4T no. 1 was built by Hohenzollern in 1903, one of six such locomotives.
Drg: J.R.

Deli Railway 'Siantar' class no. 48 was one of four 2-8-4T built by Werkspoor (417/1916) for working on the 1 in 50 Tebing-Tinggi to Siantar branch. This loco remained in service on the line throughout its working life and eventually became the last active member of the class.
Photo courtesy of Ian G.T. Duncan

Deli Railway 2-6-4T no. 54, also built by Werkspoor (467/1920), had a slightly increased coal capacity compared to the first eight members of the class built by Hartmann in 1914. These 2-6-4Ts formed the largest of the DSM's classes, amounting to 23 locos. Photo courtesy of Ian G.T. Duncan

Deli Railway no. 60, a 2-4-2T built at Hanomag in the late 1920s. Photo: author's collection.

such as 2-cylindered 0-4-4 tank engines with outside 'Allan' valve gear. All locomotives had outside cylinders and ran mainly bunker first. The large 2-8-4 tank locos were imposing engines and were called 'Siantars', predominantly hauling the heavy goods trains composed mainly of four wheeled covered wagons and palm oil and latex tank cars to Belawan-Deli, northern Sumatra's outlet to the sea on the Mallacca Straits.

An acquaintance of the writer was at the time Shedmaster at Tebing-Tinggi, a junction on the main line from Medan to Pematang-Siantar. He once furnished the writer with a set of photographs depicting the aforementioned locomotives in their original state, presumably ex-works photographs, from such firms as Werkspoor. The locomotives were provided with electric lighting at a later date. At least on one occasion the writer spotted a 'Dabeg' feed pump which was an Austrian-invented accessory, popular in that country. This was a pump mechanically driven from the locomotive's motion and consisting of 2 plunger pumps in tandem, with the exhaust steam condensing chamber in between. The one pump plunger pumped cold water into the chamber so that the spray condensed the exhaust steam and the other pump plunger pumped the hot condensate into the boiler via the usual clack valve. The cold water line had a by-pass valve and

the exhaust steam line was provided with an oil separator.

Tebing-Tinggi Junction at the time was a locomotive staging point and boasted a multiple stall engine shed with a turntable, watering facilities, and a fuel depot. Here the Siantar line branched off from the main line to Rantau Prapat. At Kisaran, another junction on the line to Rantau Prapat, a line branched off to Tandjung-Balei and further to Teluk-Nibung, both small coastal towns with access to the Malacca Straits via river mouths. Tandjung Balei possessed a prow harbour, these vessels, sail and motor driven, plying the coastal regions. Here the writer observed one of the Allan geared 0-4-4T pottering around, presumably being the branch line locomotive. Tandjung Balei boasted a 3-stall roundhouse, also with a turntable, watering facilities, and a fuel depot. The author has included a condensed diagram of this interesting layout, many such railway installations dotting the islands of Java and Sumatra, the only islands in the huge Indonesian Archipelago to possess railways, bar that part of the huge island of Borneo at the time called Brunei. The Indonesian governed part of that island is now called Kalimanten. Northern Sumatra nearly 50 years ago was a very 'steamy' area literally and figuratively with 100 percent standard 3'6" gauge steam, without a diesel in sight, and of course plantation steam too.

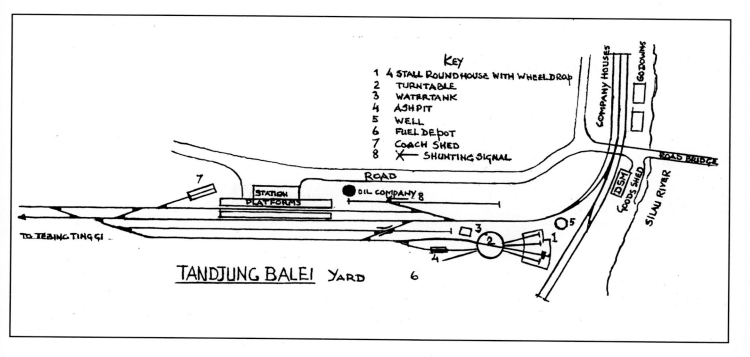

Running the Plantation Railway

The aforementioned connection with the Deli Railway Company's main line some distance away from the factories necessitated the use of transported wagons, these vehicles being low slung steel girders of 1,067 mm (3'6") gauge riding on 6-wheeled narrow gauge bogies. Lined up with the 3'6" railhead in the transport bay, they made it possible to Ro-Ro (Roll on - Roll off) standard gauge rolling stock and transport these wagons over the narrow gauge railway network to the factory either for off-loading merchandise and machinery or to load produce for shipping out. This operation ran very smoothly and the writer never heard of a transporter train toppling over.

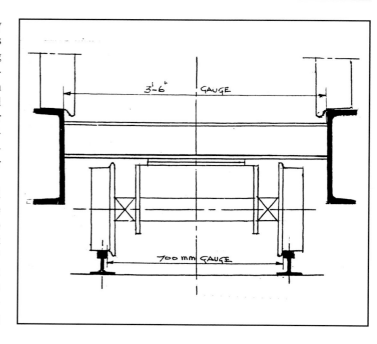

The narrow gauge and sand ballasted track was laid on local hardwood sleepers, the only wood that would stand up to the ravages of the termites. The rails were spiked down directly onto the sleepers. All narrow gauge track, however, needed constant attention with the passage of the numerous heavy 'bladtreinen' (leaf trains), trailing unsprung rolling stock, so the Eurasian ganger and his track gang had their work cut out. Track gauge was 700 mm, which was customary in the Netherlands and her oversees possessions for the narrow gauge, whilst in English speaking countries 24" (610 mm) and on the Continent 600 mm were customary.

Only the locomotives had springing, all other rail vehicles were unsprung and just bobbed along. The 'trunk lines' radiating out from the factory yard into the Plantation were at intervals provided with left or right hand turnouts to which portable track could be connected. This portable track would be laid following the topography of the land towards a section to be harvested and the loaded 4-wheeled narrow gauge rolling stock would be bullock hauled to the truck lines and there assembled into long trains to be hauled by one of the 10-couplers or Mallet Locomotives to the 'Fabriek' (Factory). The Plantation cultivated the sisal plant (Agave), with its fibrous and spiky leaves, a close non-fruit bearing relative to the fruit bearing banana tree,

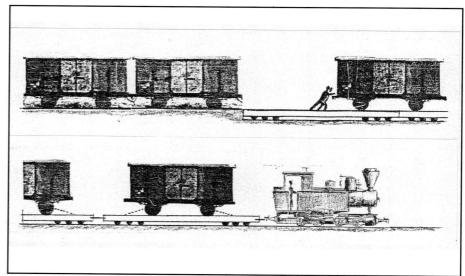

The plantation railway with bullock haulage.
Photo: author's collection.

producing Manila hemp. Both sisal fibre and Manila hemp were used for rope making and for cellulose manufacture for the explosives industry.

The 4-wheeled rolling stock, weighing in at approximately 3 or 4 tonnes fully loaded, were built out of heavy local timbers (the jungle was next door). These 4-wheeled vehicles were called 'lorries'. They were unsprung and mainly unbraked, ran on 'Panama' white metalled axle boxes, and were fitted with a centrally buffered chain and hook drawgear. The wooden underframing would have more 'give' than steel underframing when bobbing along on uneven track and repairs were easier, however, wear and tear of the built up wooden lorry was heavy and the local Chinese carpenter and his associates were forever repairing or building new rolling stock.

Incoming leaf trains were sorted out, weighed, and marshalled into the factory by an 0-4-0 Orenstein and Koppel tank locomotive, the loaded lorries being spotted alongside slatted chain conveyors taking the leaves to the 'Coronas'. These machines, with their scraper knives fitted to flywheels, de-fleshed and scraped the leaves clean using copious quantities of water and leaving the fibre bare, which then would undergo further processing, such as centrifugal drying followed by steam heat drying, combing and sorting, and finally being pressed into bales. The empty lorries were turned on small turntables and led to the 'empties' storage tracks for further despatch into the fields. The aforementioned 0-4-0T 'Teakettle'

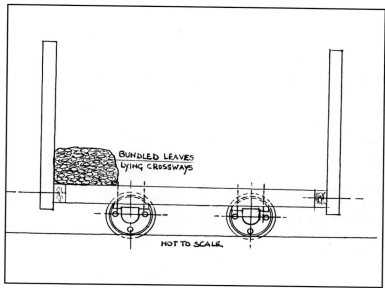

Wooden 'lorrie' for carrying sisal. Drg: J.R.

was always very busy and had the loudest bark on the system. Spotting of loaded wagons and propelling the empties out of the factory was done by human endeavour.

The locomotive stock counted a fair number of pre-war German built 0-4-0 slide valved compound Mallet tank locomo-

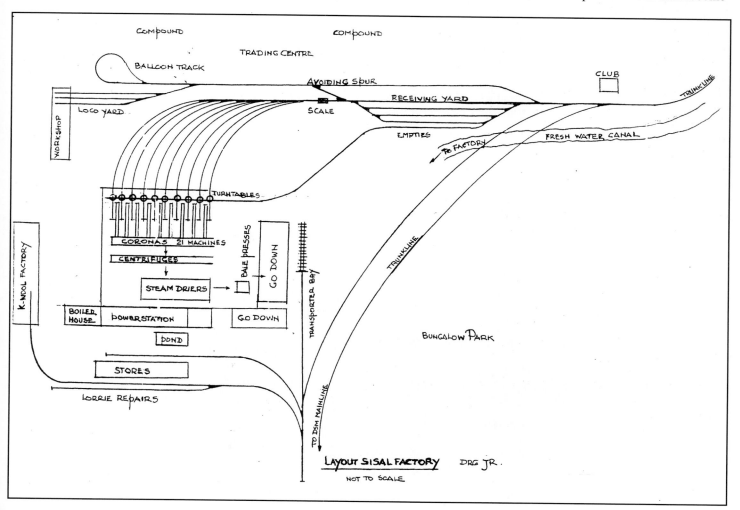

tives by Orenstein & Koppel of Berlin, with patented valve gear. Other locos were a couple of more modern post-war (1949) Ducroo & Brauns of Amsterdam 0-4-4-0 slide valved compound Mallet tank locomotives with Walschaert valve gear, and a number of rigid framed 10-coupled tender locomotives trailing a 4 wheeled tender, also constructed by Orenstein & Koppel. These last locomotives, with Walschaert valve gear, were quite modern, having piston valves, tailrodded pistons, and possessed radially adjusting axles of which more later. All locomotives were fitted with spark arrestors, were unsuperheated, had copper fireboxes and ran on residue fuel obtained from the palm oil factories.

The oil palm fruit or dates after processing and pressing in the palm oil factories produced a residue consisting of fibre and cracked shells of the pip. The oil and kernel were recovered. This residue made excellent locomotive fuel, however, somewhat dele-

terious to steel boiler plating in the long run due to its acidity, but this fact did not bother the copper fireboxes too much. Boiler water was somewhat softened with an extract (Tannin). The Mallets had displacement lubricators and the 10-couplers were provided with mechanical lubricators and carried a Duplex-steam feed pump on the running board. connected to a feedwater heater on some engines. All locomotives were fitted with steam injectors and had Johnson bar reverse levers. The Japanese Occupation used palm oil for lubricating axle boxes with some ruinous results and had the habit of destroying records. The writer has sketched out some equivalent layout from memory.

When it came to ordering new steam locomotives after the war, the Orenstein & Koppel orientated Head Office in Medan opted this time for the Ducroo & Brauns of Amsterdam 0-4-4-0 Mallet tank locomotive. The reason for this decision the writer

Du Croo and Brauns 0-8-0 Klein-Lindner tank locomotive. Photo: author's collection.

An Orenstein & Koppel Mallet compound 0-4-4-0T with outside frames for the rear, high pressure fixed unit and inside frames for the articulated low pressure unit. Drg: J.R.

can only surmise. Probably first cost and complexity had something to do with the choice of locomotive, as Klien-Lindner steam locomotives are more complex and more expensive to maintain on account of their sophisticated drive than Mallets, whose only complexity is a few ball-jointed flexible steam pipes. Possibly Orenstein & Koppel's great assembly halls were still lying in ruins after the war and the firm opted to get out of steam locomotive construction. Thus, two Mallets duly arrived in knocked down state, were set up in a few days, steamed, and then put to work.

Field personnel started their working day early in the morning by moving into the fields using motor driven 'draisines' or trolleys. These very light rail vehicles could seat 4 persons and were driven by a single cylinder Brigg & Stratton air cooled petrol engine via a belt drive. These engines toggled round a fulcrum, so tightening or slackening off the flat driving belt (see drawing). How to go about it? Start the engine with the lever in neutral and the slack belt slips on the driving pulley (vehicle stationary or stopped). Pull the lever into 'Run' (tightening the belt) and the vehicle jumps off like a spring hare (when initiated). Keep pulling the lever and a maximum speed of 30 km/hour can be maintained.

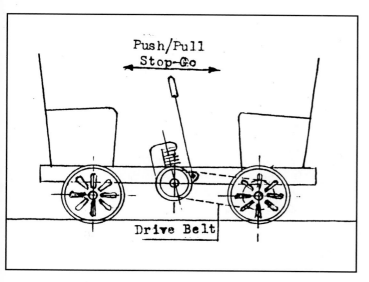

Draisine or trolley for field personnel. Drg: J.R.

To reverse the direction of running of the vehicle, simply lift the vehicle up and turn it around. Simple and ingenious. The locomotive department, as well as the workshops, had the use of a heavier ancient pre-war vehicle driven by a 4-cylinder petrol engine via a proper gearbox, but this contraption was very prone to breakdowns. If time was of no consequence, then the footplate would do. The ganger had his own spring hare. Top Brass used a jeep.

At regular intervals a 'Hospital train' was run, mostly headed by one of the agile Mallets, calling at outlying labour compounds on the Estate, catering for the ambulant sick seeking medical attention at the centrally situated hospital and for shoppers calling at the trading centre at the factory establishment. Economy class was provided on these trains by fitting a couple of lorries out with benches and roofing them over. Bouncing along at a steady 15-20 km/hour clip one would arrive at the destination thoroughly shaken, but nearly 50 years ago people were less demanding.

Shortly afterwards the writer took up an engineering post on a large oil palm plantation in a low lying coastal area of northern Sumatra. This plantation earned the sobriquet of the 'Straf Kolonie' (Penal Colony), the place being mosquito infested, stifling hot and humid, and surrounded by malarial swamps, but very interesting.

This plantation also had an extensive narrow gauge railway with many Ducroo & Brauns 8-coupled Klien-Lindner tank locomotives with separate tenders, and it had access to a DSM railhead on the standard gauge line from Tebing-tinggi to Tantau-Prapat, and standard gauge rolling stock, mainly 4-wheeled palm oil tank wagons. There must have been an agreement existing between the large plantation companies and the DSM for regular 'cosmetic' upkeep of their tank cars because workshop staff were forever busy cleaning the tank car bodywork with a soda solution and repainting in black paint. The tank car axleboxes had protective steel plates over them to ward off any palm oil spillage and cleansing soda solution.

Bunches of palm oil fruit were transported in steel baskets to the factory in the usual narrow gauge wooden framed lorries. In the factory the baskets were transferred onto steel underframed lorries and strings of these moved into autoclaves for the fruit to be pressure steamed on the stalk before being further processed. After steaming, the baskets were tipped in a rotary tippler, the stalk or stem with the fruit still attached falling into a rotary basket where the rolling action detached the softened up fruit from the stem, the fruit falling through the wide mesh of the rotating basket into a screw conveyor for despatch to the presses. The stems were used as boiler fuel. The locomotives used the residue from the presses and the shells from the pip were stored in large holding tanks and transported in rail tank cars to the Port of Belawan-Deli for shipment overseas.

The large expatriate companies have gone now, their staffs dissolved and the plantations have now become State run enterprises. The standard gauge has been de-steamed and as can be expected, most of the narrow gauge steamers have followed or will follow, as the majority of the aged engines must now be 65 years old or older, a tribute to the longevity of the steam locomotive. Whether the diesel locomotive has made inroads the writer cannot comment as he left the East-Indies in 1952 for greener pastures in southern Africa but, the trend today is to resort to trucking or tractor and trailer. Railway track also wears out. The demise of the expatriate companies also saw the demise of the locomotive building firms such as Ducroo & Brauns and Werkspoor, and many other suppliers of plantation equipment. Orenstein & Koppel of Germany ceased building steam locomotives a long time ago.

The writer after all these years still has vivid memories of giant scorpions and nasty centipedes, with their painful stings and bites, but above all of the sounds of heavily working steam locomotives coming up the rise to the 'Fabriek' with their drags in the sultry, tropical night, under the accompaniment of the racket made by troops of Howler monkeys in the nearby Sumatran Jungle.

Sugar Plantation Railways

Before ending this chapter the writer would like to briefly touch on the fourth system, namely the surrounding extensive sugar cane railways which in many respects are still extant. The

The fruit-bearing oil palm. Photo: author's collection.

island of Java had a large and thriving cane sugar industry and the vanished N.I.S. railway derived a large part of its income from this industry by transporting sugar to ports. However, this sugar industry virtually collapsed overnight after the onset of the Great Depression during the late twenties when many sugar factories closed. The author has memories of many an expatriate plantation employee having lost his job overnight. Many looked for other job opportunities and the writer can remember one man doing the circuit cutting young lads' hair. The good man knew only one hair style and that was the crewest of crew cuts, much to the glee of the school buddies.

Well remembered are the forays by bicycle into the canefields still operating, observing the diminutive plantation locomotives. These narrow gauge railways were in a world apart and quite extensive. Practically all the European narrow gauge railway equipment manufacturers were represented such as Orenstein &

Orenstein & Koppel 0-10-0 tender locomotive with Luttermöller axles. Photo: author's collection.

Koppel, Jung, and Henschel, all of Germany, and Ducroo & Brauns of Amsterdam and many more. The locomotives burned residue from the mills called Ampas (bagasse), and the tender stacked high with these bales dwarfed the actual engine. Steam - and bullock power was the mode of transport in the canefields in those days. Rolling stock comprised of the steel cane 'lorry', the wooden lorry of the Sumatran plantation as described earlier being unknown due to the dearth of suitable timber on Java. Long does the writer remember those halcyon days.

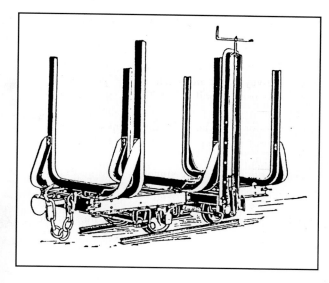

Above: A typical narrow gauge steel sugar cane wagon.

Left: A sugar factory yard with empty wagons lined up.

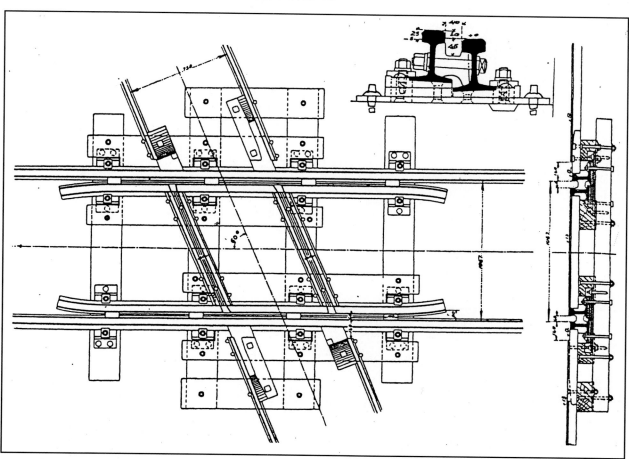

Central Java counted numerous sugar cane plantations, especially south of Djocjakarta, with many cane tramways crossing the main line. These angled crossings were called in Dutch 'Hobbel Kruisings', freely translated as 'bumpy crossings' with the main line trains thundering at speed over unbroken rails but the tramway rolling stock being human propelled or animal drawn, rocking and banging over the crossing. Locomotive power was forbidden to negotiate these crossings.

Plantation Railway Locomotive Articulation

In this final part about Indonesian plantation steam the author shall attempt to describe the origin and construction of the Klien-Lindner radially adjusting locomotive driving axles and their derivates, which at the time were a popular feature on the more powerful multi-coupled narrow gauge and plantation locomotives. This patented device was invented in Germany's State of Saxony during the last decade of the 1800s by a railway engineer named Ewald Richard Klien in conjunction with his younger colleague named Heinrich Robert Lindner. However, this clever device being somewhat heavy and costly to construct never found favour with the large railway companies at the time, who in the case of multi-coupled locomotives on curvy track opted for the more effective and less costly sideplay of driving axles as propagated by the eminent Austrian locomotive engineer Dr. Karl Gölsdorf during the first decade of the last century.

Then came along a Dr. Luttermöller, at the time a director of the locomotive manufacturers Orenstein & Koppel near Berlin in Germany, who improved on the system by driving the radially adjustable end axles via gear wheels instead of coupling rods. Orenstein & Koppel alone fitted 300 narrow gauge locomotives out with this type of axle, not to mention those constructed by that great locomotive firm of Henschel & Sohn and the Dutch manufacturers of narrow gauge railway equipment, Du Croo & Brauns of Amsterdam. The original Klien-Lindner radially adjusting axle driven by coupling rods could only be used on outside framed locomotives whilst the Luttermöller derivate made it possible to use the device on inside framed locomotives, although the ten-couplers described here and as employed on writer's plantation were outside framed locomotives with Luttermöller axles.

The outside framed device worked on "Hall" cranks, Hall being the famed English locomotive engineer who worked for the Vienna Locomotive Works in Austria round about the middle of the 1900s. Sadly the above is now obsolete technology, although re-appearing again in some form or another on modern North American Co-Co diesel

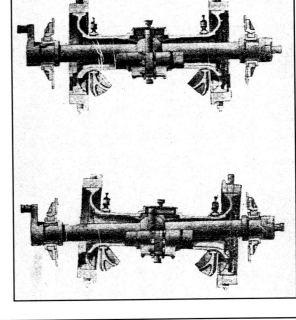

Right and below: Klien-Lindner radially adjusting axles.

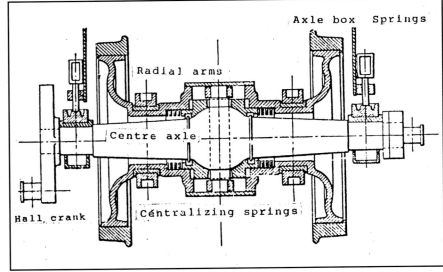

The Gölsdorf system of sideplay in axles used for Austrian 0-10-0s. The 2nd and 4th axles are rigid with the frames. Drg: J.R.

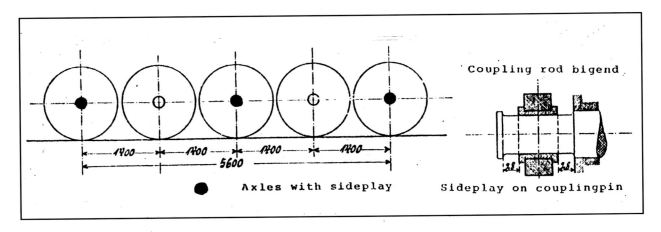

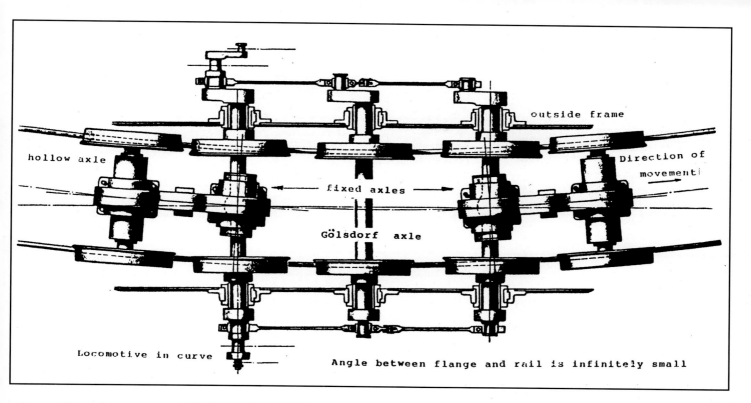

outside frame

hollow axle

Direction of movement

← fixed axles →

Gölsdorf axle

Locomotive in curve

Angle between flange and rail is infinitely small

Above: How the 0-10-0 Luttermöller design adjusts to a curved track. This diagram shows an outside framed locomotive.

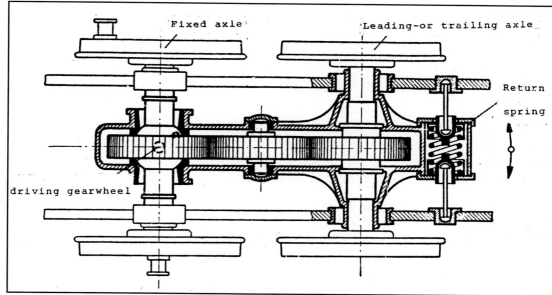

Fixed axle

Leading-or trailing axle

Return spring

driving gearwheel

Right: The Luttermöller geared drive to axles at either end of the wheelbase (inside frame locomotive).

locomotives under the guise of "steereable axles" in order to reduce flange wear on track curvature.

The Klien-Lindner radially adjusting axle consists of a central axle on which are mounted the Hall cranks and axle boxes, the locomotive weight resting on these axle boxes via springs. The axle with a globe shaped section in the centre is surrounded by a hollow divided wheelset, the two halves held together at the centre. The torque of the central axle is transmitted onto the divided wheelset via a central traction pin. The globe shaped part of the central axle makes it possible to move the hollow wheelset in any direction, within bounds, like a ball joint. Internal springs are provided for self centering. Both radially adjustable end axles are connected together by radial arms jointed in the centre.

In the case of the Luttermöller derivate the working is self-explanatory. In this case the ball-jointed movement emanates from a fixed axle in the locomotive frame, i.e. the traction pin transmits the rotation onto the 1st driving gearwheel which adjusts itself on the ball shaped axle centre.

Luttermöller radially adjusting axles were provided on all of the Estate's ten-couplers. Sometimes things went wrong with a return spring breaking and if not noticed timeously caused one of the wheel flanges of the affected axle set to run sharp, requiring extensive welding-up and re-machining of the worn wheel flange. An interesting feature on these locomotives was the way that cylinder forces were transferred onto the main crankpin, which required only one set of big end metals instead of the usual two, (see drawing). This construction also applied to the Estate's outside framed Luttermöller axled locomotives.

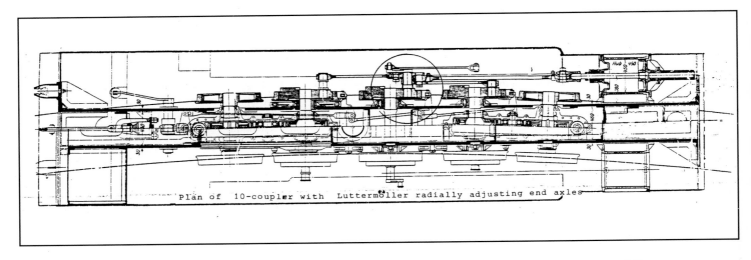

Plan of 10-coupler with Luttermöller radially adjusting end axles

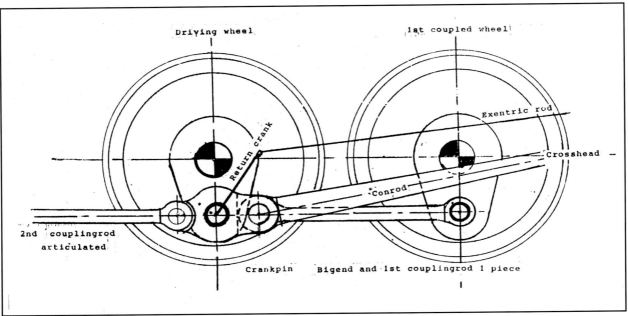

Driving wheel   1st coupled wheel

Exentric rod

Return crank

Crosshead —

Conrod

2nd couplingrod articulated

Crankpin   Bigend and 1st couplingrod 1 piece

Top: Plan of a 10-coupler engine with Luttermöller radially adjusting end axles.

Above: Diagram of the main crankpin assembly as applied to all of the Estate's 10-coupled locomotives. Note that in both diagrams the connecting rod is not driving directly onto the crankpin.
Drg: J.R.

One of the Estate's Luttermöller outside frame 0-10-0 tender locomotives, no. 38, built by Orenstein & Koppel. Photo: J.R.

The interested reader would have by now come to the conclusion that the lowly plantation steam locomotive could also show some sophistication, having five axles of which the fore and aft ones were radially adjustable, carrying electric lighting, and in many cases being fitted with feedwater apparatus like feedwater heaters and pumps. They also had mechanical lubricators and a steam distribution using modern efficient piston valves, all engineered to perfection to withstand the raw 24-hour a day "sledge-hammer" operation year in, year out.

Besides the aforementioned devices many other devices were invented in aid of getting as many wheels round the corner as possible. For example, the Austrian "Fink" system driving an extra axle via a jackshaft, or the German "Hagans" system driving an extra bogie via the main motion, or the German "Klose" system with parallelogram motion working on radially adjusting end axles, all weird and wonderful but impractical. Gölsdorf, however, made it possible to use multi-coupled locomotives like the Union Pacific's type 4-12-2. The UP were running these monsters at 60 mph whilst the nail biting Alco engineers advised not more than 30 mph. Then followed the Russian 4-14-4 which flopped, the bugbear being track spread and derailments on turnouts, but in the writer's humble opinion a front Luttermöller axle, or for that matter a fore & aft one, would have cured the problem and most likely the locomotive would have been saved for posterity. Perhaps the Russians did not wish to pay out royalties but that is conjecture. A fascinating subject.

Luttermöller 0-10-0T+T no. 263 of P.G. Ngadirejo sugar mill, Java, seen on 18th September 1983 with the tender piled high with bagasse. The loco was built by Orenstein & Koppel (11618/1928). Photo: Phil Gilbert.

A typical Indonesian plantation locomotive, 700 mm gauge Mallet compound 0-4-4-0T no. 68, built in Holland by Du Croo & Brauns and owned by the Dolok Sinumbah estate situated in the Siantar region of Sumatra. Photo: A.E. Durrant.